Übernachten in China

Sleepover in China

Edition **DETAIL**

Individuell und oft im Bestand: Übernachten in China

Individual Designs in Existing Building Stocks: Sleepover in China

Der White Pagoda Temple Hutong in Beijing gehört zu den wenigen traditionellen Wohnquartieren der Stadt, die überlebt haben. Erdgeschossige Hofhäuser reihen sich dort entlang der engen Gassen mit ihrem geschäftigen Leben. In einer etwas ruhigeren Seitenstraße verweist nur die rostbraune Eingangstür aus Stahl zwischen dem grauen Mauerwerk auf das kleine Boutique-Hotel. Über einen Durchgang gelangt der Besucher in den Innenhof, der die einzelnen Gästezimmer erschließt. Jedes davon ist individuell gestaltet und führt uns ein räumliches Experiment vor Augen, vor allem aber offenbart es die Lust seiner Entwerfer an wohlüberlegten trendigen Ausbaudetails. Alt und Neu harmonieren hier auf gelungene Weise. Etwa 1500 Kilometer südlich, im Hinterland von Jiangxi, zeigt sich ein ähnliches Bild: In einem 300 Jahre alten Holzhaus haben Architekten und Betreiber ein stilvolles Gästehaus eingerichtet, das Geschichte und Atmosphäre ausstrahlt; auch hier sind die neuzeitlichen Zutaten liebevoll integriert, auch hier spielen Tradition und modernes Design perfekt zusammen. Das sind nur zwei von zahlreichen Beispielen für kleine, spezifisch gestaltete Hotels, wie sie aktuell in ganz China entstehen.

Nach wie vor aber gehört für viele Beobachter eine exklusive Architektur nicht gerade zu den ersten Attributen, die sie spontan mit dem Land verbinden. Denn viel zu grau und monoton zeigt sich das übliche Baugeschehen fast überall, und so haben sich die Massen an billigen und einförmigen Wohn- und Büroblocks, die das Bild der meisten Städte prägen, in unseren Köpfen festgesetzt.
Seit einigen Jahren jedoch ist die Szene enorm in Bewegung. Eine neue Architektengeneration tritt auf die Bühne. Es ist die erste Generation, deren führende Protagonisten mehrheitlich im Westen ausgebildet sind, und der es nun möglich ist, private Büros zu betreiben. Anders als die Architektur der gigantischen staatlichen Planungskonglomerate, die lange Zeit den Markt allein beherrschten, zeichnen sich ihre Entwürfe durch individuelle Herangehensweisen, das bewusste Reagieren auf den jeweiligen Kontext sowie den sensiblen Umgang mit Material und Raum aus. Mit ihren meist kleinen Projekten versuchen Chinas neue Architekten, einen gesellschaftlichen Mehrwert zu generieren oder an die kulturelle Tradition ihrer Heimat anzuknüpfen. Noch eine weitere Besonderheit indes fällt auf: Zahlreiche ihrer Projekte befinden sich auf dem Land, viele auch im Bestand. Beides war noch vor wenigen Jahren die absolute Ausnahme.

SANFTER TOURISMUS STATT LANDFLUCHT

Lange Zeit konzentrierte sich das Baugeschehen in China fast ausschließlich auf die großen Städte. Infolge des unvergleichlichen Wirtschaftsaufschwungs ab den 1980er-Jahren strömten die Menschen zu Hunderten von Millionen aus den ländlichen Gebieten dorthin, um in den Metropolen ihr Glück zu versuchen. Abertausende von Dörfern verfielen. Denn auch die Zurückgebliebenen wollten nicht länger in den alten Bauernhäusern aus Lehm und Holz leben. Sie galten als unzeitgemäß, boten zu wenig Komfort und wurden folglich durch meist gesichtslose Neubauten ersetzt. Parallel dazu wurde auch in den Städten der überlieferte Baubestand flächendeckend niedergewalzt, um den Neuankömmlingen, vor allem aber dem vermeintlichen Fortschritt Platz zu machen. So ging ein erheblicher Teil der baulichen Tradition des Riesenreichs in nur wenigen Jahrzehnten unwiederbringlich verloren.
In allerjüngster Zeit aber findet ein Umdenken statt. Architekten ebenso wie die Vertreter der regionalen Verwaltungen besinnen sich auf ihr baukulturelles Erbe und versuchen davon zu erhalten, was nur irgendwie geht. Parallel setzt die Regierung nun alles daran, die massive Landflucht zu bremsen und initiiert Projekte, die dazu beitragen sollen, die Lebensqualität und die wirtschaftliche Situation der Menschen in den Dörfern zu verbessern, nicht selten durch die Förderung eines sanften Tourismus. In nur wenigen Jahren sind auf diese Weise im ganzen Land in unzähligen Bauernhäusern Gästezimmer oder kleine, familiengeführte Hotels entstanden, die dazu beitragen, die vernakuläre Architektur zu erhalten und der ansässigen Bevölkerung eine zusätzliche Einnahmequelle zu sichern.
Das verdeutlicht nicht zuletzt das auch international beachtete Beispiel von Songyang in der Provinz Zhejiang, wo die Landkreisverwaltung zusammen mit der Beijinger Architektin Xu Tiantian eine

The White Pagoda Temple Hutong in Beijing is one of the few traditional residential quarters of the city that have survived. Here, ground-level courtyard houses are strung out along the narrow lanes with their busy activity. In a quieter side street, only a rust-brown steel entrance door in between the grey masonry indicates the small boutique hotel. A passage leads visitors to the courtyard, which provides access to the individual guestrooms. Each has been individually designed and illustrates a spatial experiment. Above all, however, it reveals the designers' delight in well-thought-out, trendy finishing details. Here, the old and the new harmonise successfully.

A similar picture emerges about 1,500 kilometres to the south, in the hinterland of Jiangxi: in a 300-year-old timber building, a stylish guesthouse was set up by the architects and operators, exuding a sense of history and an ambience; here too, modern elements have been lovingly integrated in a perfect interplay of tradition and contemporary design.

These are only two of many examples for small, specifically-designed hotels that are currently emerging all over China.

Exclusive architecture may, however, not exactly be among the first things many observers spontaneously associate with the country. This is because the usual building activity almost everywhere seems much too grey and monotonous, with the bulk of cheap, uniform residential and office blocks, which characterise the image of most cities, lodging itself in our minds.

However, for several years now, a lot has been going on in the scene. A new generation of architects has emerged. It is the first generation whose leading protagonists have predominantly been educated in the West, and for whom it is now possible to run private offices. Unlike the architecture of the gigantic governmental planning conglomerates, which for a long time had dominated the market, their designs are characterised by individual approaches, deliberate responses to the respective context, as well as the sensitive handling of materials and spaces. With their mostly small-scale projects, China's new architects are attempting to generate an added social value or to take up the cultural tradition of their homeland. Another particularity should also be noted: a large number of their projects are located in the countryside, and many in existing building stocks, too. Both were highly unusual even only a few years ago.

GENTLE TOURISM INSTEAD OF RURAL FLIGHT

For a long time, building activity in China almost exclusively focused on the large cities. As a result of the unparalleled economic boom from the 1980s onwards, people thronged there from rural regions in their hundreds of millions to try their luck in the metropolises. Thousands upon thousands of villages decayed, since even those who stayed back no longer wanted to live in the old farmhouses made of loam and timber. These were considered outmoded, offered too little comfort, and were therefore replaced by mostly faceless new buildings. At the same time, the traditional building stock in the cities, too, was flattened across large areas to make room for the newcomers and, above all, for supposed progress. Hence, a considerable part of the architectural tradition of the huge country was irretrievably lost in only a few decades.

Most recently, however, a rethink has been taking place. Architects as well as representatives of the regional administrations are refocusing on their architectural heritage and trying to preserve whatever possible. Simultaneously, the government is now making every effort to limit the massive migration from the land and is initiating projects which are aimed at improving the quality of life and the economic situation of the people in the villages, often by supporting gentle tourism. In this way and in only a few years, guestrooms or small family-run hotels have been created in countless farmhouses all over the country, making a contribution to the conservation of the vernacular architecture and ensuring an additional source of income for the local population.

This is, not least, illustrated by the example of Songyang in Zhejiang, which has also been noted internationally, and where the district administration, together with the architect Xu Tiantian from Beijing, initiated many specific interventions. Alongside spectacular museums or visitor centres, these also include community facilities as well as various redevelopments of localities, and linked to these, the integration of so-called homestays in old buildings in the villages.

Vielzahl gezielter Interventionen initiierte. Neben spektakulären Museen oder Besucherzentren gehören dazu auch Gemeinschaftseinrichtungen sowie verschiedene Ortssanierungen und damit verbunden die Integration sogenannter Homestays in alten Häusern in den Dörfern.

INDIVIDUALITÄT WIRD GROSS GESCHRIEBEN

Doch was wäre das Angebot ohne die Nachfrage? Es trifft sich in diesem Zusammenhang gut, dass Chinas rasant wachsende Mittelschicht aus den Metropolen gerade das Land für sich entdeckt. Zumindest, um dort für ein paar Tage Urlaub zu machen oder über das Wochenende dem Smog und dem Trubel der Großstadt zu entfliehen. Und wenn man sich schon aufs Land begibt, soll die Atmosphäre möglichst authentisch sein. Das Übernachtungsangebot in alten Gemäuern aus Lehm kommt dazu gerade recht. Natürlich nur unter der Voraussetzung, auf den von zu Hause gewohnten Komfort nicht verzichten zu müssen. Gleichzeitigt entsteht unter den Bürgern der neuen Mittelschicht ein immer größeres Bedürfnis nach Individualität als verständliche Reaktion auf die jahrzehntelange Gleichschaltung der Massen. Nun versucht, wer es sich leisten kann, aus der Gleichförmigkeit auszubrechen – sei es, um Eigenständigkeit und den damit verbundenen Wohlstand zu demonstrieren oder um einem echten persönlichen Bedürfnis zu folgen. Auf dieses Verlangen reagieren die individuell gestalteten Unterkünfte.
Längst ist es kein Geheimnis mehr, dass weltweit Hotels mit ihrer Ausstattung auf die rapide um sich greifende Selfie-Kultur und die damit verbundene Selbstdarstellung im Internet reagieren. Kein Wunder, denn deren »Instagrammability«, also die Tauglichkeit, in sozialen Netzwerken damit zu punkten, wird laut Umfragen für viele, vor allem junge Leute, bei der Hotelwahl zunehmend bedeutender und rangiert mittlerweile vor angesagten Sehenswürdigkeiten in der Umgebung. Nirgendwo aber ist die Netztauglichkeit so wichtig wie in China, nirgendwo sonst greift die Selfie-Kultur gleichermaßen um sich, verbunden mit dem ständigen Posten auf WeChat, der chinesischen Mischung aus WhatsApp, Instagram und Twitter, über die jeder ständig mit jedem verbunden ist. So wird das Hotel selbst zunehmend zum eigentlichen Ziel der Reise. Das fördert den Wunsch nach individuell gestalteten, manchmal auch ausgefallenen Räumen. Von der neuen Vielfalt profitieren dann auch andere Reisende, denen zuallererst an Land und Leuten oder einfach nur an ein paar Tagen entspannter Erholung gelegen ist. Schließlich war gerade in China das Spektrum lange Zeit enorm begrenzt. Parallel zu dem Angebot an eigenständigen Übernachtungsmöglichkeiten hat sich in nur einem Jahrzehnt auch das Angebot an Verkehrsmitteln enorm verbessert; so überzieht heute ein dichtes Netz an Hochgeschwindigkeitszügen das Land, mit denen man oftmals auch den entlegensten Winkel erreicht.

AUF DEM LAND ODER INMITTEN DER STADT

Die meisten der in diesem Buch vorgestellten Hotels befinden sich in Altbauten, auf dem Land wie in der Stadt. Damit bieten sie oft die ideale Voraussetzung, um neben Kultur und Sehenswürdigkeiten auch die traditionelle Architektur Chinas zu erleben.
Schauen wir dazu zuerst nach Wuyuan. Hier, im Hinterland der Provinz Jiangxi, existieren noch zahlreiche traditionelle Dörfer mit Gebäuden im typischen Huizhou-Stil, der auch in den angrenzenden Regionen in Anhui und Zheijiang verbreitet ist und als Inbegriff der ländlichen Architektur aus der Zeit der Ming- und Qing-Dynastie gilt. Dicht gedrängt stehen in den kleinen Ortschaften dort die prächtigen Hofhäuser aus Holz, umschlossen von dicken, weiß verputzten Mauern und mit schweren Ziegeldächern gedeckt. Ein solches Haus im Dorf Yan hat sich ein junges Aussteigerpaar aus der Finanz- und Designwelt von Shanghai gekauft, um darin fortan das mit 14 Zimmern ausgestattete Wuyuan Skywells Hotel zu betreiben (Seite 20). Zuvor aber galt es, das stark in Mitleidenschaft gezogene Gebäude möglichst originalgetreu wiederherzustellen. Wertvolle Hilfe leistete dabei der buchstäblich letzte und bereits sehr alte Zimmermeister in der Region, der als einziger noch Erfahrung im Bau solcher Häuser hatte. Während der Sanierung brachte er nicht nur sein Wissen und seine Fertigkeiten ein, sondern gab sie damit zugleich an die nächste Generation weiter. So wurde das Hotelprojekt einerseits zum Katalysator für die

Umnutzung im traditionellen Bestand in Stadt und Land.

Oben: Das Layering Courtyard Hutel in einem ehemaligen Hutong in Beijing.

Unten: Beim Tsingpu Tulou Retreat zeigen die Altbauten mit ihrer einfachen Holzkonstruktionen und Wänden aus Stampflehm eine große Rustikalität.

Reutilisation of traditional buildings in the city and the countryside.

Above: The Layering Courtyard Hutel in a former Hutong in Beijing.

Below: In the Tsingpu Tulou Retreat by Hua Li/TAO, the old buildings with their simple timber structures and walls of rammed clay display a high rustic quality.

örtliche Wirtschaft und trug andererseits dazu bei, die alte Handwerkskunst am Leben zu halten. Ebenso führt es den anderen Hausbesitzern im Dorf vor Augen, wie ein altes Gebäude sinnvoll erhalten werden kann, statt es wie lange Zeit üblich nur abzureißen und durch einen Neubau zu ersetzen. Den Gästen aber bietet der Aufenthalt im Skywells Hotel die besondere Gelegenheit, ein traditionelles chinesisches Hofhaus von innen heraus zu erleben. Die malerischen Orte und die ländliche Ruhe der Umgebung gibt es selbstredend dazu.
Auch beim Tsingpu Tulou Retreat in Taxia in der Provinz Fujian geht es darum, alte Gebäude zu bewahren und gleichzeitig einen sanften Tourismus zu fördern (Seite 88). Ganz in der Nähe des Orts befinden sich einigen der bekanntesten als »Tulou« bezeichneten gigantischen Lehmburgen der Hakka, die dem gemeinschaftlichen Wohnen eines ganzen Klans dienen und sich durch große Rustikalität auszeichnen. Ihre massiven und bis zu zwei Meter dicken Mauern aus Stampflehm wirken abweisend und uneinnehmbar, sind ausgewaschen und zeigen Risse. Die dahinterliegende Holzkonstruktion wirkt schwer, besticht aber durch ihre strukturelle Einfachheit. Filigrane Schnitzereien wie an den Häusern in Wuyuan sucht man hier vergebens. Ähnlich präsentieren sich auch die kleineren Hofhäuser im Dorf Taxia, von denen drei den Kern des Hotels bilden. Bei ihrer Gestaltung gelingt es dem Architekten Hua Li, einem der führenden Vertreter seiner Zunft in China, beispielhaft, mit nur wenigen subtilen Eingriffen den ländlichen Charakter komplett zu erhalten und trotzdem ein Luxusresort zu kreieren. Wohl kein anderes Hotel der gehobenen Kategorie im Land strahlt gleichermaßen viel bäuerliche Atmosphäre aus, und trotzdem muss der Gast bei seinem Aufenthalt nicht auf einen hohen Komfortstandard verzichten.

IM HOFHAUS ODER INDUSTRIEDENKMAL

Hofhäuser gehören zur chinesischen Baukultur ebenso wie deren Tragwerke aus Holz. Traditionell finden sie sich in allen Regionen vom hohen Norden bis in den tiefsten Süden, auf dem Land sind sie gleichermaßen verbreitet wie in der Stadt. So bestand auch Beijing einmal fast ausschließlich aus dicht aneinandergebauten Hofhäusern. In den wenigen verbliebenen Hutong-Quartieren dort haben sich zahlreiche kleine Hotels und Herbergen angesiedelt. Lange Zeit bedienten die meisten davon mit ihrer Ausstattung – roten Laternen im Freibereich und reichlich Plüsch und Schnitzwerk im Inneren – den populären Geschmack des Durchschnittsreisenden. Seit aber in allerjüngster Zeit auch Architekten die Aufgabe für sich entdeckt haben, entsteht eine Reihe von Umbauten mit hohen gestalterischen Ansprüchen, wobei viele davon ihren besonderen Reiz gerade aus dem Zusammenspiel von Alt und Neu beziehen. Das trifft auch auf das eingangs erwähnte privat betriebene kleine Design-Hotel im White Pagoda Temple Hutong zu, wobei »alt«, zumindest was die reine Bausubstanz betriff, dort gerade einmal sieben Jahre meint (Seite 76). Denn auch in den bestehenden Hutongs wurde der überwiegende Teil der Gebäude in jüngster Zeit auf Druck der Regierung nach und nach mit dem Argument der besseren Standsicherheit und der Verbesserung hygienischer Verhältnisse erneuert – oftmals in der ursprünglichen Größe und Form. Jedoch durfte bei der Sanierung die Baukörperform sowie die Materialität zum Außenraum aus Denkmalschutzgründen nicht angetastet werden. Wie schon das klassische Hofhaus erhält nun auch der Umbau seinen besonderen Charme aus dem spannungsvollen Kontrast zwischen der harten Schale aus Mauerwerk und schweren Ziegeldächern sowie dem weichen Kern mit viel Holz und Glas zum Hof. Stärker noch wirkt dieser Kontrast beim »Layering Courtyard« getauften Hutel Guesthouse, das ebenso in einem Hutong-Quartier entstand, allerdings in einem weit größeren, ehemals kommerziell genutzten Gebäude (Seite 82). Hier konnten die Architekten einen transparenten neuen Flügel komplett aus Stahl und Glas in dem umbauten Freibereich platzieren, sodass ein mehrschichtiger Hof entsteht, in dem die Privatheit durch teilweise Bedruckung der Gläser vom Eingang bis zum rückwärtigen Haus mit den Gästezimmern kontinuierlich zunimmt. Trotz der beengten Situation zeigen sich alle Gemeinschaftsräume angenehm hell und bestechen durch das reizvolle Zusammenspiel zwischen den klaren modernen Materialien sowie dem warmen, dunklen Holz der beeindruckenden, zum Innenraum offenen alten Dächer.

INDIVIDUALITY IS A PRIORITY

What would, however, supply be without demand? In this context, it is convenient that China's rapidly growing middle class from the metropolitan cities is currently discovering the countryside for itself – at least for going on holiday there for a few days or escaping from the smog and hustle and bustle of the metropolis over a weekend – and if one is going to the countryside, the atmosphere should be as authentic as possible. For this purpose, overnight accommodation in old loam buildings turns out to be just right, under the condition of not having to dispense with the comfort familiar from home.
At the same time, the citizens of the new middle class have a growing desire for individuality, an understandable response to the decades-long enforced conformity of the masses. Those who can afford it, are now trying to overcome the uniformity, be it to display individuality and – linked to this – affluence, or to follow a genuine personal desire. The individually designed accommodations respond to this wish.
It is no secret that hotels worldwide are adapting their facilities in response to the rapidly proliferating selfie culture and the internet-based self-portrayal linked to it. No wonder, since their "instagrammability", i.e. their suitability for scoring in social networks, is, according to surveys, becoming more important for many people when selecting a hotel, especially for young persons, and in the meanwhile ranks before trendy attractions in the surroundings. Nowhere else, however, does web suitability seem as important and the selfie culture to be proliferating as rapidly as in China, in conjunction with continuous postings on WeChat, the Chinese blend of WhatsApp, Instagram, and Twitter, continuously connecting everyone. The hotel itself thus increasingly becomes the actual purpose of a trip. This supports the desire for individually designed and sometimes also unusual spaces. The new diversity benefits other travellers too, who are, first and foremost, interested in the country and its people or simply in a few days of relaxation. After all, particularly in China, the range in this regard was very limited for a long time.
Alongside the availability of individual overnight accommodation, the availability of means of transport has also enormously improved in only one decade; for example, a dense high-speed train network covers the country today, often linking even the most remote corners.

RURAL LIFE OR IN THE MIDST OF THE CITY

Most of the hotels presented in this book are located in old buildings, both in the countryside and the city. They therefore often provide ideal conditions for experiencing the traditional architecture of China alongside the culture and sights.
Let us look at Wuyuan in the first instance. Here, in the hinterland of the province of Jiangxi, many traditional villages with buildings in the typical Huizhou style still exist, which is also found in the neighbouring regions of Anhui and Zhejiang, and is considered to be the embodiment of rural architecture from the time of the Ming and Qing dynasties. Splendid timber-built courtyard houses are densely packed within small localities here, enclosed by thick, white-plastered walls and with heavy brick roofs. Such a house, in the village of Yan, was purchased by a creatively-minded young couple from the financial and design sectors of Shanghai, to henceforth operate the 14-room Wuyuan Skywells Hotel (page 20) in it. First, however, the rundown building had to be renovated as true to the original as possible. Valuable help came from literally the last and already very old master carpenter in the region, who was the only one to still have experience in the construction of such houses. During the renovation, he not only applied his knowledge and skills but, in doing so, also passed them on to the next generation. The hotel project thus, on the one hand, became a catalyst for the local economy, and on the other, contributed to keeping the old craftsmanship alive. At the same time, it has made the other house owners in the village aware of how an old building can be meaningfully preserved, instead of simply tearing it down – as was common for a long time – and replacing it with a new building. Guests staying at the Skywells Hotel have the special opportunity of experiencing a traditional Chinese courtyard house from the inside. The scenic places and the rural serenity of the surroundings are, of course, part of the experience.
In the Tsingpu Tulou Retreat in Taxia, too, located in the province of Fujian, the objective is to preserve old buildings and simultaneously encourage

Umnutzung im industriellen Bestand auf dem Land und in der Stadt. Oben: Das Alila Yangshuo Hotel von Vector Architects besticht durch seine fantastische Lage direkt am Li-Fluss. Unten: Neri&Hu inszenieren mit The Waterhouse in Shanghai den Verfall eines ehemaligen Lagerhauses regelrecht.

Reutilisation of industrial buildings in the city and the countryside. Above: The Alila Yangshuo Hotel by Vector Architects impresses with its fantastic location directly on the banks of the River Li. Below: With The Waterhouse in Shanghai, Neri&Hu downright choreographed the decay of a former warehouse.

gentle tourism (page 88). Close to the locality, some of the most well-known gigantic and fortified loam dwellings of the Hakka can be found, known as "Tulou", which serve as community housing for an entire clan and are distinguished by a high degree of rusticity. Their solid, up to two-metre-thick walls of rammed earth appear unapproachable and impenetrable, and are washed out, while also showing cracks. The timber construction placed behind them seems heavy is captivating due to its structural simplicity. There are no delicate carvings, as found on the houses in Wuyuan. A similar picture emerges with the smaller courtyard houses in the village of Taxia, of which three form the core of the hotel. In their design, the architect Hua Li, one of the leading representatives of his profession in China, succeeded and completely preserving the rural character in an exemplary manner, using only a few subtle interventions, while still creating a luxury resort. Perhaps no other hotel in the upscale category in the country exudes as much rural atmosphere, while guests don't have to dispense with a high standard of comfort during their stay.

COURTYARD HOUSE OR INDUSTRIAL MONUMENT

Courtyard houses, just as their timber load-bearing structures, are a part of Chinese building culture. Traditionally, they are found in all regions from the high north to the deepest south, and they are as widespread in the countryside as in the city. Beijing, too, once almost exclusively consisted of densely adjoined courtyard houses. Here, in the few remaining Hutong quarters, many small hotels and hostels have been established. For a long time, most of these catered to the popular taste of the average traveller, with furnishings that included, for example, red lanterns in open areas and plenty of plush and carvings in interiors. However, since architects have also discovered this task for themselves, a series of building conversions with high design requirements is taking place, and many of these derive their special charm precisely from the interplay of the old and the new. This also applies to the small, privately run design hotel in the White Pagoda Temple Hutong mentioned at the start, where "old" means to refer to just seven years, at least with respect to the actual building stock (page 76), since in the existing Hutongs too, the major part of the buildings was gradually renovated due to pressure from the government, with the rationale of improved structural safety and hygienic conditions – often in the original size and form. However, due to heritage conservation reasons, the shape of the building structure as well as the materiality towards the outside space were not to be touched during the renovation. As was already the case with the classic courtyard house, the new building now also derives its special charm from the suspenseful contrast between the hard shell comprising masonry and heavy tiled roofs as well as the soft core with an abundance of wood and glass towards the courtyard.

This contrast has an even stronger impact in the Hutel Guesthouse, dubbed Layering Courtyard, which was likewise created in a Hutong quarter, albeit in a far larger, formerly commercially used building (page 82). Here, the architects were able to place a transparent new wing, made entirely of steel and glass, in the built-up open area, resulting in a multilayered courtyard, where privacy continually increases due to partially printed glass panes as one goes from the entrance to the house with the guestrooms in the rear. In spite of the spatially confined situation, all common spaces are pleasantly bright and captivating, with the charming interplay between the clear, modern materials and the warm, dark timber of the impressive old roofs, which are open towards the interior.

The building stock in the hotel The Waterhouse at the South Bund in Shanghai (page 92), comprising a somewhat minor warehouse, doesn't offer such features but others instead. The architects Lyndon Neri and Rossana Hu masterfully understood how to present these. Their objective was not to make a traditional built form perceptible, as is the case with many of the above-described hotel projects. Instead, they attempted to preserve the visible decay in the form of crumbling concrete and paint residues on the walls, utilising its sensuous qualities as a backdrop for a refined design. At the same time, they allowed the building, which is typical for the former port area, to tell its story. When The Waterhouse opened in 2011, it was the first design hotel in China to cause an international sensation. However, it was also one of the very first buildings here that illustrated a rethink in handling building stocks.

The Alila Hotel in Yangshuo, which was completed in late 2017, has also caused a stir around the

Derartige Qualitäten kann der Baubestand – ein eher unbedeutendes Lagerhaus – beim Hotel The Waterhouse am South Bund in Shanghai nicht bieten (Seite 92). Dafür aber andere, und die Architekten Lyndon Neri und Rossana Hu verstehen es meisterhaft, diese in Szene zu setzen. Ihnen geht es nicht darum, eine überlieferte Bauform erlebbar zu machen, wie es bei vielen der oben beschriebenen Hotelprojekte der Fall ist. Stattdessen versuchen sie, den sichtbaren Verfall in Form von bröckelndem Beton und Farbresten an den Wänden zu konservieren und dessen sinnliche Qualitäten als Hintergrund für edles Design zu nutzen. Gleichzeitig lassen sie das Haus, das typisch für die ehemalige Hafengegend ist, damit seine Geschichte erzählen. Als The Waterhouse 2011 eröffnet wurde, war es das erste Design-Hotel in China, das international Furore macht. Es gehörte aber auch zu den allerersten Bauten dort, die ein Umdenken im Umgang mit dem Bestand demonstrierten.
Nicht weniger weltweite Beachtung findet aktuell das Ende 2017 fertiggestellte Alila Hotel in Yangshuo (Seite 124). Auch hier bildet ein ehemaliger Industriebau den Kern. Doch befindet sich dieser nicht in der Großstadt, sondern abgelegen in einer der spektakulärsten Landschaften Chinas. Jahrelang waren die Gebäude der früheren Zuckermühle aus den 1960er-Jahren stillgelegt und verlassen, bis sie ein Projektentwickler durch Zufall entdeckte und dann zusammen mit Gong Dong von Vector Architects das Konzept für ein Luxushotel entwickelte. Der Architekt brachte dabei alle öffentlichen Funktionen von der Rezeption bis zu Restaurant oder Bibliothek im Bestand unter und entwarf sorgfältig eingefügte neue Gebäude von hoher gestalterischer Qualität für die Gästezimmer und Suiten. So überzeugt die Gesamtanlage durch das perfekte Zusammenspiel von Alt und Neu, aber auch von Architektur, Innenraumdesign und Freiflächengestaltung. Nicht zuletzt bezieht das Alila Yangshuo seinen besonderen Reiz aus der fantastischen Lage direkt an dem in ganz China berühmten Li-Fluss mit den malerischen Karstbergen. Abertausende von Touristen kommen jährlich hierher, um sie zu bewundern – auf der Terrasse am Swimmingpool des Hotels befindet sich der Gast bereits mittendrin.

Doch zurück in die Stadt oder besser gesagt in die weit ausufernden Vororte der Sechs-Millionen-Metropole Hangzhou zu dem vielleicht eigenwilligsten Gästehaus in diesem Buch. Auch Hangzhou war einmal für die landschaftliche Schönheit seiner Umgebung bekannt. Wenn auch heute vor Ort an vielen Stellen zwischen den ausufernden sterilen Neubauten nicht mehr viel davon zu spüren ist, zeugen doch unzählige traditionelle Gemälde und Gedichte davon. Auf solche klassischen Landschaftsbilder und die darin enthaltene Poesie bezieht sich Wang Shu, der Pritzker-Preisträger von 2012, oftmals mit seinen Projekten. So entwirft er auch das zwischen einem grünen Hügel und einem kleinen Fluss am Rand des schon Jahre zuvor von ihm geplanten Xiangshan Campus der Kunstakademie gelegene Wa Shan Guesthouse wie eine künstliche und begehbare Landschaft und inszeniert vor allem die Wege durch das Haus, die zum räumlichen Erlebnis werden (Seite 114).
Das Wa Shan Guest House von Amateur Architecture Studio gehört zu der kleinen Gruppe von nur vier vorgestellten Neubauten in diesem Buch. Das verdeutlicht, wie wichtig die Auseinandersetzung mit dem überlieferten Baubestand urplötzlich in China wird. Es zeigt aber auch, wie gut sinnvoll integrierte Gästehäuser oder kleine Hotels zu dessen Erhalt und damit auch zum Überleben der regionalen Baukultur beitragen können. Fast alle behandelten Gebäudebeispiele sind klein, einige verfügen gar über weniger als zehn Gästezimmer. Trotzdem reicht die Bandbreite von der einfachen Herberge zum Luxusresort, vom Land über die Kleinstadt bis in die Metropolen. Ganz bewusst ist dabei das Spektrum auch in angrenzende Bereiche erweitert, die Beispielsammlung enthält auch eine Jugendherberge sowie als extreme Position das Micro-Hutong-Projekt von ZAO/standardarchitecture als Konzeptstudie für ein mögliches Hostel. Alle vorgestellten Architekten haben ihren Bürositz in China. Neben einigen jungen sind fast alle großen Namen darunter, von Zhang Ke bis Hua Li, von Gong Dong bis Wang Shu oder Neri&Hu. Auch das veranschaulicht, wie vielfältig und zeitgemäß die Planungsaufgabe gerade ist. Keine andere Typologie repräsentiert die aktuelle Architektur in China im Moment umfassender als die individuell gestalteten kleinen Hotels.

Christian Schittich

world (page 124). Here too, a former industrial building forms the core. It is, however, not located in a large city but lies remotely in one of the most spectacular landscapes of China. For years, the buildings of the former sugar mill from the 1960s had been disused and abandoned until a project developer discovered them by chance, and then, together with Gong Dong of Vector Architects, developed the concept for a luxury hotel. In doing so, the architect accommodated all public functions in the building stock, from the reception to the restaurant and the library, and designed carefully incorporated new buildings of high design quality for the guestrooms and suites. The overall complex is thus convincing due to the perfect interplay between the old and the new, but also between architecture, interior design, and the design of open spaces. The Alila Yangshuo derives its special charm also from its fantastic location directly by the banks of the River Li, well-known all over China, and the scenic karst mountains. Thousands upon thousands of tourists come here every year to admire them – on the terrace by the hotel's swimming pool, guests are already right in the middle.

However, reverting to the city, or rather to the widely overflowing suburbs of the metropolis of Hangzhou with its six million inhabitants, we come to perhaps the most idiosyncratic guesthouse in this book. Hangzhou, too, was once known for the beauty of its surrounding landscape. Even though in many locations amidst the mushrooming, sterile new buildings, not much of this seems to be perceivable anymore, countless traditional paintings and poems are proof thereof. Wang Shu, the Pritzker Prize laureate in 2012, often refers to such classic landscape images, and the poetry they contain, in his projects. He also designed the Wa Shan Guesthouse, located between a green hill and a small river on the outskirts of the Academy of Art's Xiangshan Campus, which he had planned years earlier, as an artificial and walkable landscape, particularly choreographing the paths through the building that form a spatial experience (page 114).

The Wa Shan Guesthouse by Amateur Architecture Studio belongs to the small group of only four new buildings presented in this book. This illustrates how important the debate on the traditional building stock is suddenly becoming in China. However, it also shows how well sensibly integrated guesthouses or small hotels can contribute to its preservation and hence also to the survival of regional building culture.

Almost all presented building examples are small, with some even having fewer than ten guestrooms. Nevertheless, the spectrum ranges from a simple hostel to a luxury resort; from the countryside via the small town to the metropolitan cities. In doing so, the range has been deliberately extended to adjoining areas – the collection of examples also contains a youth hostel and, as an extreme position, the Micro Hutong project by ZAO/standardarchitecture, as a concept study for a possible hostel.

All presented architects have their offices in China. Alongside some young ones, almost all major names are represented, from Zhang Ke to Hua Li, from Gong Dong to Wang Shu or Neri&Hu.

This, too, illustrates how diverse and topical the planning task currently is. No other typology represents current architecture in China more comprehensively than the individually designed small hotels.

Christian Schittich

Projekte

Projects

Guojiaguo 6
Beijing 11 12 16
Yangzhou 13
Nanjing
Shanghai 14 15 19
Chengdu
Mogan Shan 5
Daomingzhen 7
Hangzhou 18
Wuyuan 1
Pingtian 2
Dali 8
Kunming
Fuzhou
Nanjing 3
Yangshuo 4 20
Xiamen 9 10
Shenzhen 17

Landleben

Country Life

Wer ein traditionelles chinesisches Hofhaus erleben will, ist im Wuyuan Skywells Hotel genau richtig. Außen dicke, weiß verputzte Mauern, die die Hitze abhalten und Schutz bieten, innen ein Kern aus Holz und in der Mitte ein enger Hof mit Brunnen. Er ist schmal genug, um die direkte Sonneneinstrahlung fernzuhalten, lässt aber über die Dächer genug Regen herein. Denn das Wasser, das über den »Himmelsbrunnen« (skywell) in das Haus kommt, ist nicht nur ein lebensnotwendiges Gut, sondern bringt der Überlieferung zufolge auch Wohlstand und Glück. Drei solcher Höfe hat das Gebäude, das sich ein junges gemischtethnisches Paar kaufte, um es wieder herzurichten und darin nun ein Hotel zu betreiben.
Unbehandeltes Holz ist das bestimmende Material im Inneren, überall liegt dessen angenehmer Geruch in der Luft. Die traditionelle Dachkonstruktion ist in den Gästezimmern offen sichtbar, die Einrichtung, teilweise aus alten Möbeln, dazu passend und stilvoll. Notwendige Ergänzungen zeigen sich zurückhaltend modern.
Das kleine Restaurant befindet sich in einem dezenten Anbau aus Stahl und Glas, der von außen betrachtet hinter der hohen Gartenmauer verschwindet. Hier genießen die Gäste ihr Frühstück mit Zutaten aus der Region: Reissuppe und Reiskuchen mit eingelegtem Gemüse, Teigtaschen mit würziger Fleischfüllung, dazu gekochten Mais und scharf gewürzte Bohnen. Anschließend geht es auf geliehenen Fahrrädern in die stimmungsvollen Dörfer der Umgebung. Tiefer im Land kann man im Osten Chinas kaum irgendwo sein. Entsprechend ruhig ist es nachts. Nur gelegentlich bellt ein Hund, und früh am Morgen wird der Reisende vom Krähen des Hahns geweckt.

For those who wish to experience a traditional Chinese courtyard house, the Wuyuan Skywells Hotel is just the right place to do so. With thick, white plastered walls on the outside, which keep out the heat and provide protection, and a core made of timber, the centre comprises a small courtyard with a well. The courtyard is narrow enough to avoid direct sunlight while letting in sufficient rain via the roofs, as the water, that enters the house through the skywell not only is a vital commodity but also brings prosperity and happiness, according to tradition. The building, with three such courtyards, was purchased by a young, mixed-ethnic couple who renovated it and now run a hotel in it.
Untreated wood is the predominant material inside, with its pleasant smell infusing the air everywhere. The traditional roof construction is readily visible in the guestrooms, accompanied by fitting and stylish furnishings partly consisting of old furniture. Necessary additions have been designed in a restrained modern manner.
The small restaurant is housed in an understated annex made of steel and glass, which disappears behind a high garden wall when viewed from the outside. Here, guests can enjoy their breakfast, prepared with ingredients from the region: rice soup and rice cakes with pickled vegetables, dumplings with spicy meat filling, accompanied by cooked maize and hot beans. Afterwards, bicycles can be rented tovisit the impressive villages in the surrounding area. There is hardly a place in eastern China more deeply immersed in the countryside than here. At night, it is correspondingly quiet; only occasionally, a dog can be heard barking, and early in the morning, travellers are awakened by the crows of a cock.

Ort: Wuyuan/Jiangxi
Architekten: Andreas Thomczyk, Mika Woll, Amy Mathieson/ anyScale
Bauherr: Edward Gawne, Selina Liao
Zimmer: 14

Location: Wuyuan/Jiangxi
Architects: Andreas Thomczyk, Mika Woll, Amy Mathieson/ anyScale
Client: Edward Gawne, Selina Liao
Rooms: 14

Schnitt/Grundriss
Maßstab 1:400
1 Rezeption
2 Restaurant
3 Hof (Skywell)
4 Gästezimmer
7 Küche
11 Swimmingpool (geplant)

Section/Floor Plan
scale 1:400
1 Reception
2 Restaurant
3 Courtyard
4 Guestroom
7 Kitchen
11 Swimming pool (projected)

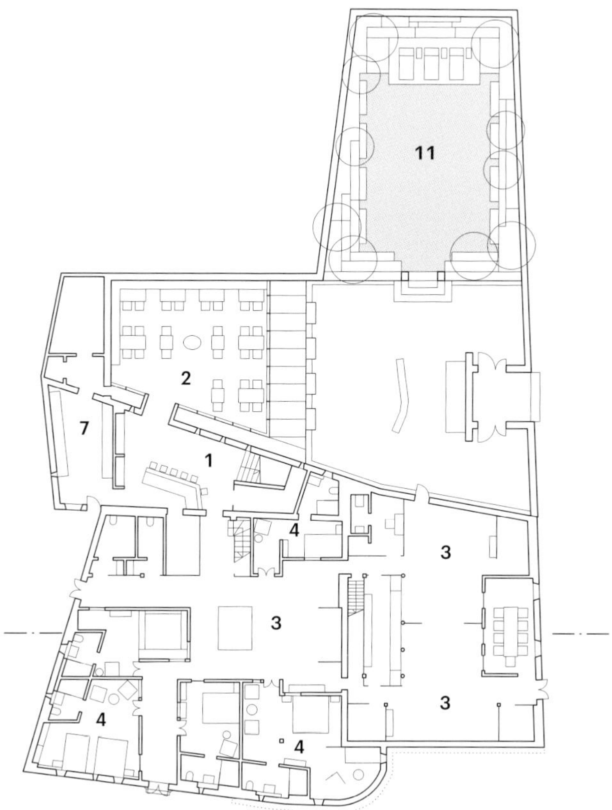

Ein Dorf als Hotel

A Village as Hotel

Die Ortssanierung von Pingtian gehört zu einem ambitionierten Katalog an gezielten Eingriffen in verschiedenen Gemeinden, die die Landkreisverwaltung von Songyang initiiert hat, um durch Förderung eines sanften Tourismus die Lebensqualität auf dem Land zu verbessern. Das kleine Dorf mit seinen traditionellen Häusern aus Stampflehm und Holz liegt malerisch auf einer Bergkuppe und ist von terrassierten Teeplantagen, Gemüsefeldern und Bambushainen umgeben. Im Zuge des Projekts wurden unterschiedliche Gebäude saniert und mit neuen Nutzungen versehen. Unter anderem hat die Beijinger Architektin Xu Tiantian in einer Hausgruppe ein kleines Museum für landwirtschaftliche Geräte nebst Handwerkszentrum eingerichtet.

Den zentralen Bestandteil des Vorhabens aber bildet das Pingtian Cloud Village Hotel, das der Architekt Wang Weijen aus Hongkong über verschiedene Bestandsbauten entlang des steil ansteigenden Dorfwegs anordnete, um es komplett in die gewachsene und authentische Dorfstruktur zu integrieren. Seinen Kern bildet ein prototypisch wiederhergerichtetes Hofhaus, das nun als Restaurant dient. Im Haus darüber sind die Rezeption, ein Ausstellungs- und Verkaufsraum für örtliche Produkte sowie einige der Hotelzimmer untergebracht. Die anderen Gästeräume sowie ein Teepavillon sind auf weitere kleine Häusern verteilt.

In all diesen Gebäuden hat der Architekt behutsam moderne Materialien wie Glas und Stahl integriert und in Beziehung zu den überlieferten Baustoffen Bambus, Lehm und Holz gesetzt. Gleichzeitig lenken bewusst platzierte Öffnungen in den massiven Außenmauern den Blick in den Ort oder die nahen Berge.

The redevelopment of Pingtian is part of an ambitious array of specific interventions in various communities, which the district administration of Songyang has initiated to improve rural quality of life by supporting gentle tourism. The small village, with its traditional houses of rammed earth and timber, picturesquely lies on a hilltop and is surrounded by terraced tea plantations, vegetable fields, and bamboo groves. In the course of the project, different buildings were renovated and given new uses. Among other things, the architect Xu Tiantian from Beijing has installed a small museum for agricultural equipment, along with a crafts centre, in a group of buildings.

The main part of the project, however, is the Pingtian Cloud Village Hotel, which the architect Wang Weijen from Hong Kong accommodated in various existing buildings along the steeply ascending village road, in order to completely integrate it into the evolved and authentic village structure. Its core comprises a prototypically restored courtyard house, which now serves as a restaurant. The building above accommodates the reception, an exhibition and salesroom for local products, as well as some of the hotel rooms. The other guestrooms and a tea pavilion are spread across further small buildings.

In all these buildings, the architect carefully integrated modern materials such as glass and steel, and thoughtfully combined them with the traditional materials bamboo, clay, and timber. At the same time, deliberately placed openings in the solid external walls direct the view to the locality or the nearby mountains.

Ort: Pingtian/Zhejiang
Architekten: Wang Weijen Architecture
Bauherr: Jiang Binlong/Pingtian Cloud Village Hotel

Location: Pingtian, Zhejiang
Architects: Wang Weijen Architecture
Client: Jiang Binlong/Pingtian Cloud Village Hotel

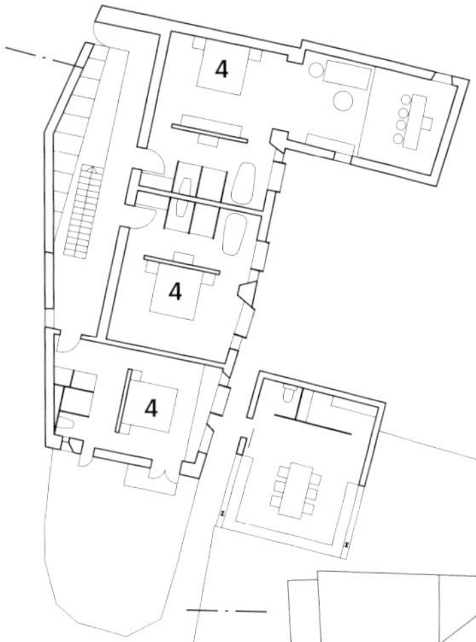
4
4
4

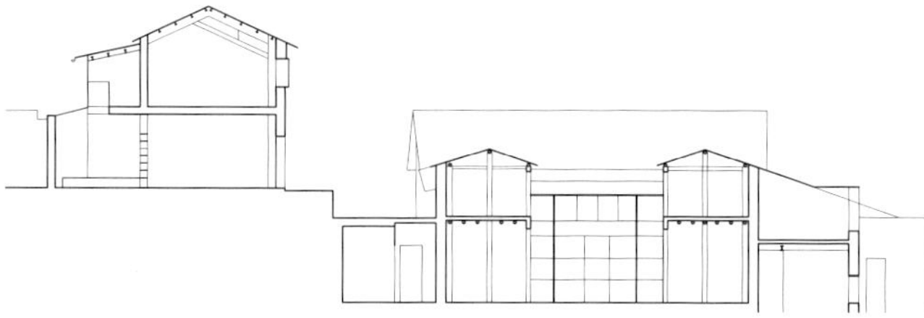

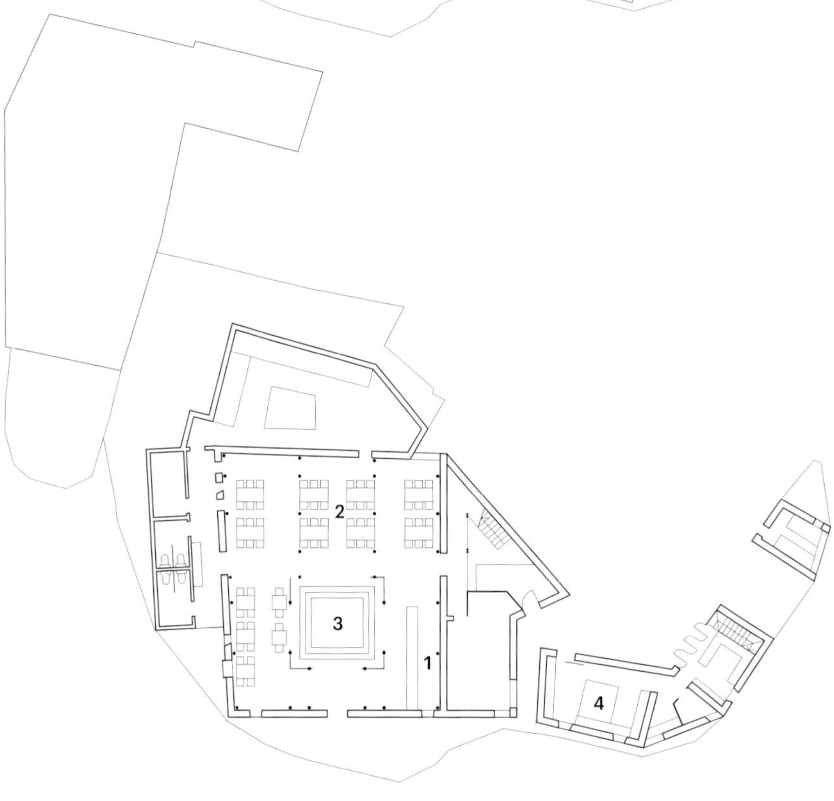
2
3
1
4

Grundrisse/Schnitt
Maßstab 1:400
1 Rezeption
2 Restaurant
3 Innenhof
4 Gästezimmer

Floor Plans/Section
scale 1:400
1 Reception
2 Restaurant
3 Courtyard
4 Guestroom

Lageplan
Maßstab 1:1500
A Empfang/Gastronomie
B Teepavillon
C Gästezimmer
D Jugendherberge
E Hostel
F Künstleratelier
G Museum

Site plan
scale 1:1,500
A Reception/Restaurant
B Tee Pavilion
C Guestrooms
D Youth Hostel
E Hostel
F Studios
G Museum

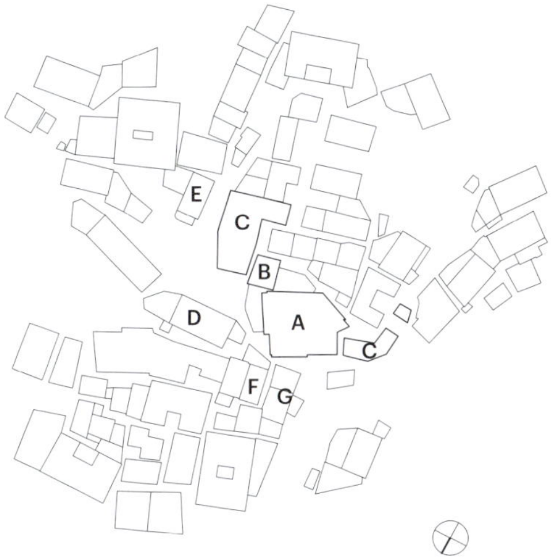

Luxus auf dem Bauernhof

Luxury on the Farm

Der Geruch von frischem Gras und Holz liegt in der Luft, Stampflehm und rauer Stein prägen die Außenwände: Für Gäste, die die bäuerliche Kultur in China auf höchst komfortable Art erleben wollen, wurde das Tsingpu Tulou Retreat geschaffen, das sich in dem Dorf Taxia im Süden von Fujian über ein größeres Gebäude aus dem frühen 20. Jahrhundert sowie verschiedene alte Bauernhäuser erstreckt. Diese werden ebenso als »Tulou« – Haus aus Lehm – bezeichnet wie jene gigantischen Gemeinschaftsbauten der Hakka, für die die Region berühmt ist und von denen einige ganz in der Nähe des Hotels als Unesco-Weltkulturerbe registriert sind. Den ursprünglichen Charakter von Dorf und Gebäuden soweit wie möglich zu erhalten, hatte bei der Umnutzung für den Architekten Hua Li und die Betreiber die höchste Priorität.
So entstand ein Luxushotel, das mit seinem Ort und der regionalen Kultur auf maximale Weise verwurzelt ist. Kleinere Ergänzungsbauten wie Rezeption und Restaurant wurden mithilfe traditioneller Materialien gefühlvoll eingepasst, auch die Bodenbeläge in den Freibereichen spiegeln örtliche Traditionen wider. Schadhafte Holzteile im sichtbaren Tragwerk wurden durch jahrhundertealte Balken aus Abbruchhäusern der Umgebung ersetzt, das warme, rustikale Material prägt die Atmosphäre der Räume. Der stilvolle Ausbau strahlt eine zeitgemäße Eleganz aus und passt sich dennoch perfekt ein.
Auch über die Architektur hinaus hat sich das Hotel der regionalen Hakka-Kultur verschrieben. Das schlägt sich in den angebotenen Speisen ebenso nieder wie in Workshops zu traditioneller Malerei auf Holz, zu Keramik und Scherenschnitt oder zur Teeerzeugung.

The scent of fresh grass and wood fills the air, while rammed earth and rough stone characterise the external walls of the Tsingpu Tulou Retreat, which was created for guests who wish to experience rural culture in China most comfortably. The retreat is located in the village of Taxia in southern Fujian, and extends across a larger building from the early 20th century as well as various old farmhouses. These are likewise called "Tulou", loam house, as are the gigantic community buildings of the Hakka, for which the region is famous, with some in the vicinity of the hotel registered as UNESCO world cultural heritage. For the architect, Hua Li, and the operators, the highest priority was to preserve the original character of the village and the buildings during the conversion as far as possible.
This resulted in a luxury hotel rooted in its location and the regional culture to a maximum extent. Smaller supplementary buildings, such as the reception and restaurant, were sensitively incorporated with the aid of traditional materials, while the floor coverings in the open areas also reflect local traditions. Defective timber components in the exposed load-bearing structure were replaced by centuries-old beams from demolished buildings in the surrounding area, with the warm, rustic material shaping the atmosphere of the spaces. The stylish finishing exudes a contemporary elegance while still perfectly fitting in.
Even going beyond the architecture, the hotel has committed itself to the regional Hakka culture. This is likewise reflected in the dishes on offer as well as the workshops on traditional painting on wood, ceramics, paper cut, or the production of tea.

Ort: Taxia/Fujian
Architekten: Hua Li/TAO (Trace Architecture Office)
Bauherr: Beijing Origin Inn Group
Zimmer: 22

Location: Taxia, Fujian
Architects: Hua Li/TAO (Trace Architecture Office)
Client: Beijing Origin Inn Group
Rooms: 22

Schnitt, Lageplan
Maßstab 1:750
1 Rezeption/Lobby
2 Restaurant
3 Hof
8 Seminarraum
17 Tulou
18 Bach

Section/Site plan
scale 1:750
1 Reception/Lobby
2 Restaurant
3 Courtyard
8 Seminar room
17 Tulou
18 Stream

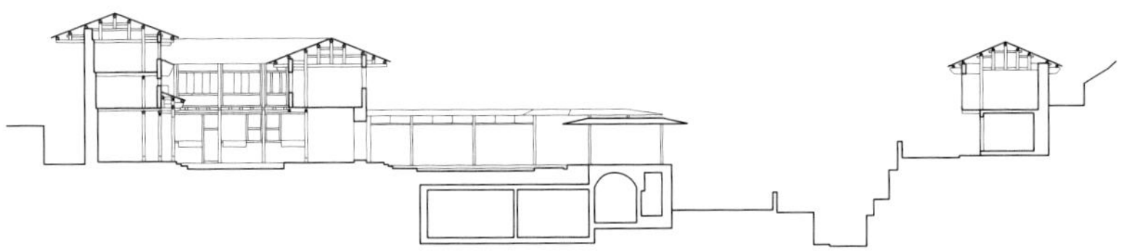

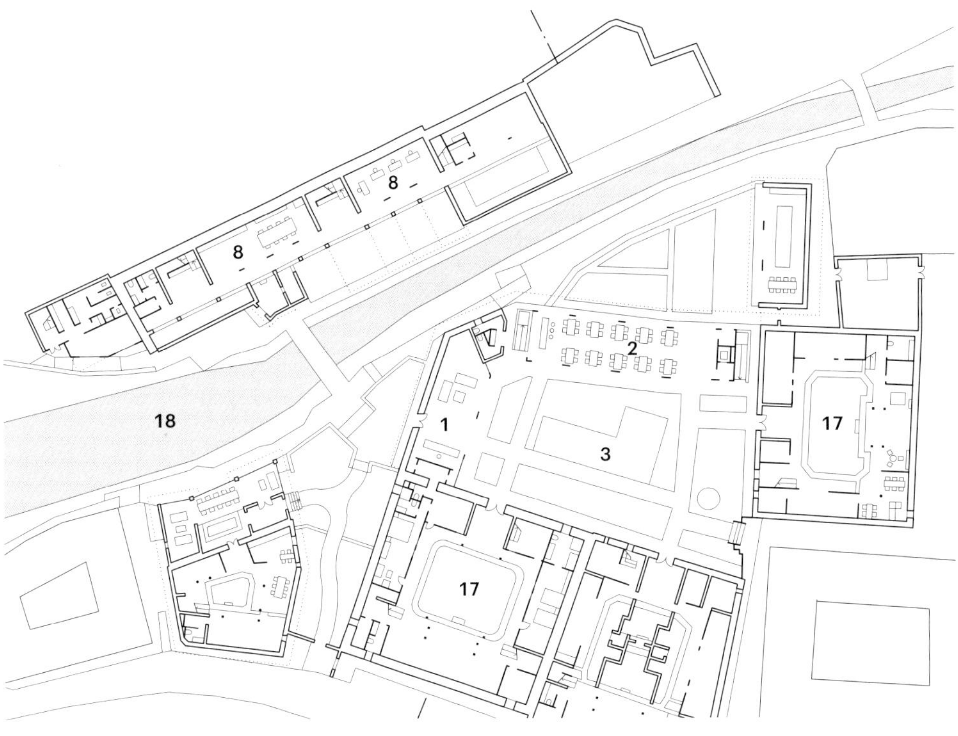

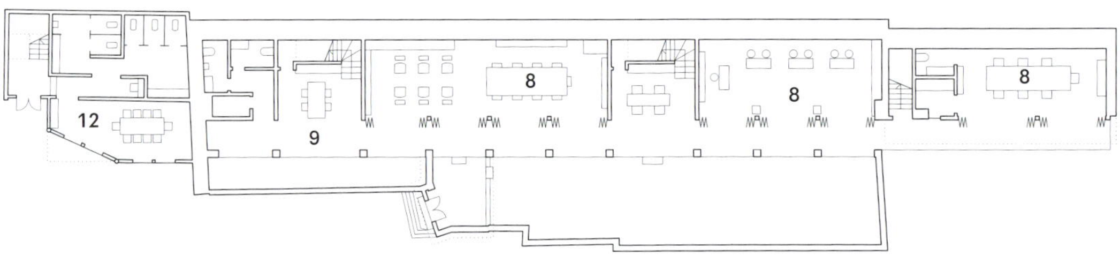

8
12
9
8
8

Grundrisse
Maßstab 1:400
3 Hof
4 Gästezimmer
8 Seminarraum
9 Bibliothek
12 Personal

Floor Plans
scale 1:400
3 Courtyard
4 Guestroom
8 Seminar room
9 Library
12 Staff

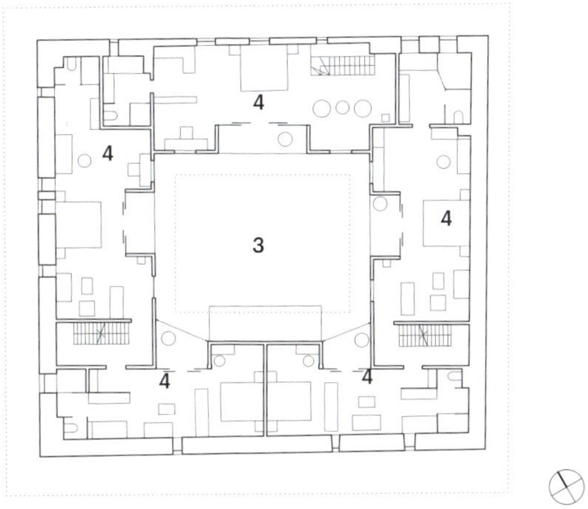

Komfort im Lehmziegelhaus

Comfort in a Mud-Brick Building

Perfekter kann sich ein Hotel auf dem Land kaum in seine Umgebung integrieren: Als Teil einer gewachsenen Dorfstruktur belegt das Yun House entsprechend seiner Philosophie, einen nachhaltigen Tourismus zu fördern, fünf ehemalige Bauernhäuser aus Stampflehmziegeln. Direkt daneben wird auch tatsächlich noch Landwirtschaft betrieben. Schade nur, dass der restliche Ort, obwohl weitab vom Schuss, zunehmend aus hässlichen Neubauten besteht. So fühlt sich der Gast beim Betreten des Hotelareals wie in einer anderen Welt, denn hier sind die alten Häuser liebevoll restauriert und die Ergänzungsbauten wie das kleine Restaurant, das auf regionale Küche Wert legt, in Material und Größe behutsam eingefügt. Bei der Aufteilung der Bestandsbauten in komfortable Gästeapartments behielten die Architekten deren ursprüngliche dreizonige Gliederung bei. So sieht der typische Grundriss in der Mitte einen hohen, bis unter das offene Holzdach reichenden Wohnbereich vor und rechts und links davon je zwei Schlafräume auf zwei Etagen. Damit ist die Unterkunft nicht zuletzt für Familien oder größere Gruppen geeignet.

Die Innenraumgestaltung zeigt sich weniger stringent als in vergleichbaren Boutique-Hotels, ist aber angenehm. Als Highlight erweist sich der nachträglich etwas erhöht am Hang angelegte Swimmingpool. Umrandet von üppigem Bambus kann man hier mit Blick auf die eindrucksvollen Karstberge seine Bahnen ziehen. Nur wenige Kilometer vom Hotel entfernt befindet sich eines der spektakulärsten Landschaftspanoramen entlang des berühmten Li-Flusses, das auch die Rückseite des 20-Yuan-Scheins ziert.

There is hardly a hotel that is more perfectly integrated into its rural surroundings: as part of an evolved village structure, the Yun House, in accordance with its philosophy to support sustainable tourism, occupies five former farmhouses made of rammed earth bricks. Right beside them, agriculture is still actually practiced. It's just a pity that the remaining place, though far off the beaten track, increasingly consists of unsightly new buildings. On entering the hotel area, guests therefore feel like they're stepping into another world, as the old buildings have been lovingly restored here, and the supplementary buildings, such as the small restaurant, which attaches importance to regional cuisine, have been delicately incorporated with respect to their material and size. While converting of the existing buildings into comfortable guest flats, the architects retained their original three-zoned structure. The typical floor plan thus has a high, centrally located living room, reaching right up to the open timber roof, with two bedrooms each on its left and right, located on two storeys. This makes the accommodation particularly suitable for families or larger groups.

The interior design is less stringent than in comparable boutique hotels, but pleasant. A highlight is the swimming pool, which was added later and is located a little higher on a slope. Framed by lush bamboo, one can swim laps with a view of the impressive karst mountains. Only a few kilometres from the hotel, one of the most spectacular landscape panoramas unfolds along the famous River Li, which also adorns the rear side of the 20 yuan note.

Ort: Yangjia Village/Guangxi
Architekten: Liu Yuyang Architects, Ares Partners
Bauherr: XY Yun House

Location: Yangjia Village/Guangxi
Architects: Liu Yuyang Architects, Ares Partners
Client: XY Yun House

Grundrisse
Maßstab 1:1000
1 Empfang/ Rezeption/Lobby
2 Restaurant
4 Gästezimmer
5 Gruppen-/ Familienapartment
6 Lounge
9 Bibliothek
11 Swimmingpool

Floor Plans
scale 1:1,000
1 Front desk/ Reception/Lobby
2 Restaurant
4 Guestroom
5 Group/family flat
6 Lounge
9 Library
11 Swimming pool

Wasser als Designkonzept

Water as Design Concept

Der Nationalpark Moganshan in Zheijiang, etwa 200 Kilometer südwestlich von Shanghai und nur 60 Kilometer von der Provinzhauptstadt Hangzhou entfernt und damit gut für einen Ausflug über das Wochenende geeignet, gehört zu den beliebtesten landschaftlichen Attraktionen in China. Dunst umhüllte Berge, dichte Bambuswälder und weitläufige Teeplantagen prägen das Bild. So überrascht es nicht, dass dort in den vergangenen Jahren besonders viele individuell gestaltete Hotels und Gästehäuser entstanden sind.

Das Anadu Resort versteht sich selbst als Luxusherberge für einheimische wie ausländische Urlauber, die abseits der Metropolen in einer intakten ländlichen Umgebung entspannen wollen. Diese so wenig wie möglich zu beeinträchtigen, gehört zu seiner Grundphilosophie. So versuchen die Betreiber und Architekten bei den im Restaurant angebotenen Speisen ebenso wie bei den zum Bau verwendeten Baumaterialien soweit wie möglich auf Produkte aus der Region zurückzugreifen. Bambus und dunkles Holz setzen im Innenraum Akzente zu den hellen Flächen aus Beton oder Putz und prägen das Bild der edlen Gestaltung.

Zentrales Element des Hoteldesigns aber sind die Wasserflächen auf den Dächern, die die insgesamt nur vier Gästezimmer umgeben. Sie strahlen Ruhe aus, erzeugen ein Gefühl von Entspannung und binden die einzelnen Teile der Anlage zusammen. Darüber hinaus bildet das natürliche Element einen fließenden Übergang in die umgebende Landschaft.

Moganshan National Park in Zhejiang, about 200 kilometres south-west of Shanghai and only 60 kilometres from the provincial capital, Hangzhou, and hence well-suited for a weekend trip, is one of the most popular scenic attractions in China. Mist envelops the mountains, with dense bamboo forests and extensive tea plantations characterising the view. It is, therefore, not surprising that a particularly large number of individually designed hotels and guesthouses have come up here in recent years.

The Anadu Resort understands itself as a luxury hotel for local and foreign holidaymakers who want to relax in an intact rural environment away from the metropolitan cities – affecting the environment as little as possible is part of its basic philosophy. The operators and architects have therefore made an attempt to draw on products from the region, in both the cuisine at the restaurant and the building materials used for construction. Bamboo and dark wood are highlights of the interior design, juxtaposed with bright surfaces made of concrete or plaster, defining the refined design as a whole.

However, the central element of the hotel design is formed by the water surfaces on the roofs, which surround a total of only four guestrooms. They exude calm and create a sense of relaxation, while tying together the individual parts of the complex. In addition, the natural element forms a fluent transition into the surrounding landscape.

Ort: Huzhou/Zhejiang
Architekten: Studio 8
Bauherr: Anadu
Zimmer: 4

Location: Huzhou/Zhejiang
Architects: Studio 8
Client: Anadu
Rooms: 4

Grundrisse
Maßstab 1:400
1 Empfang/ Rezeption/Lobby
4 Gästezimmer
6 Lounge/Bar/ Frühstücksraum
11 Swimmingpool
13 Terrasse/Balkon

Floor Plans
scale 1:400
1 Front desk/ Reception/Lobby
4 Guestroom
6 Lounge/Bar/Breakfast room
11 Swimming pool
13 Terrace/Balcony

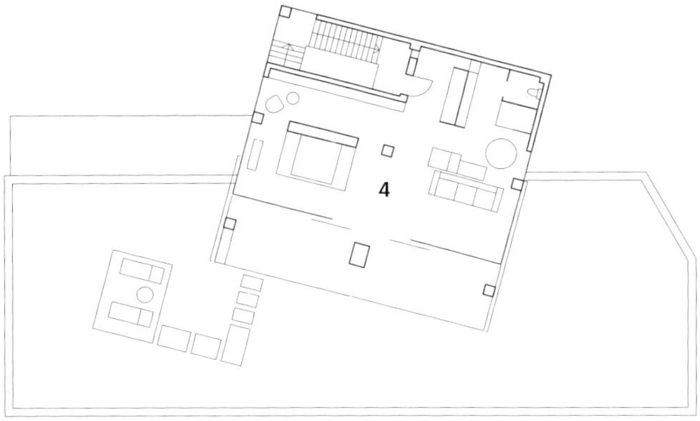

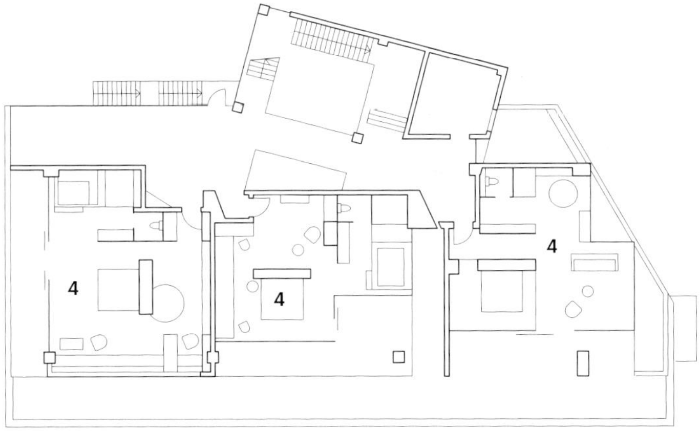

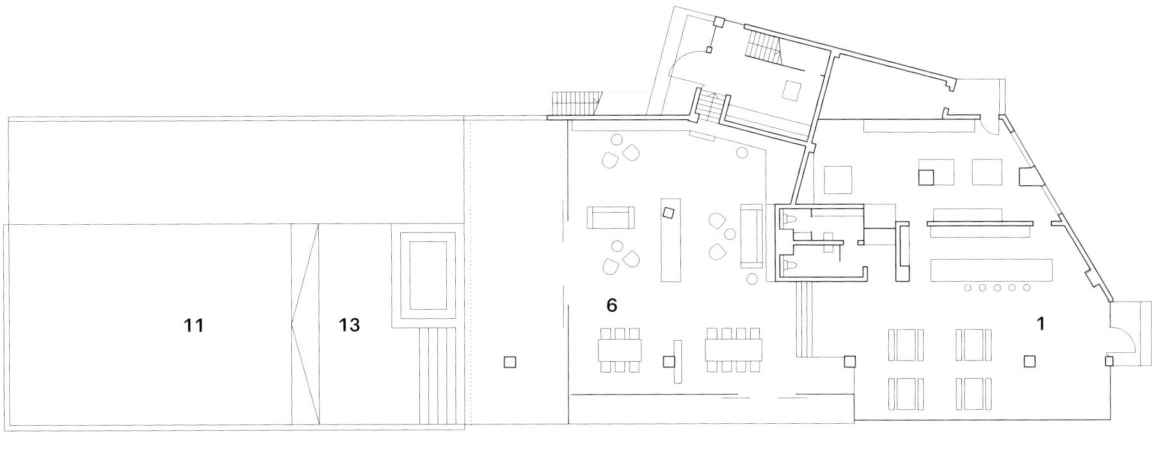

Landleben mit Komfort

Country Life with Comfort

Unter Chinas rasant wachsender Mittelschicht in den Metropolen entsteht zunehmend der Wunsch, ein paar Tage im Jahr auf dem Land zu verbringen. Die gestressten Großstadtmenschen wollen in der Zeit so ursprünglich wie möglich wohnen und der Natur möglichst nahe sein, dabei aber auf die gewohnten Annehmlichkeiten nicht verzichten. Genau dieses Bedürfnis will das Bed & Breakfast nur eine Autostunde östlich von Beijing am Rand eines kleinen Dorfs erfüllen. Seinen Kern bildet ein knappes Dutzend eingeschossiger Häuser aus dem in Nordchina üblichen dunkelgrauen Mauerwerk, bedeckt mit schweren Ziegeldächern. Diese Altbauten binden die Architekten mit einer modernen, weiß gehaltenen Konstruktion aus Stahl, Glas und Beton zusammen, die perfekt mit dem rauen Bestand korrespondiert und dessen sinnliche Qualitäten unterstreicht. Gleichzeitig schaffen sie damit verschiedene zusätzliche Räume sowie ein überdachtes halböffentliches Wegesystem, das die einzelnen Zimmer erschließt. Das Zentrum der Anlage bildet der aus dem Bestand übernommene Innenhof, um den alle gemeinschaftlichen Einrichtungen wie Rezeption und Foyer, Restaurant und Frühstücksraum angeordnet sind. Die unterschiedlich großen Gästezimmer und Apartments sind alle hell und geschmackvoll gestaltet und verfügen jeweils über einen eigenen gefassten Freibereich, der zu einer der beiden von viel Grün umgebenen Wasserflächen orientiert ist. So lässt sich die Natur mit allem Komfort im Rücken erleben.

China's rapidly growing middle class in the metropolitan cities increasingly desires to spend a few days a year in the countryside. During this time, stressed big-city dwellers wish to live as primordially and be as close to nature as possible, while not having to forego habitual conveniences. It is precisely this desire that the bed & breakfast, only an hour's drive east of Beijing on the outskirts of a small village, wishes to fulfil. Its core comprises nearly a dozen single-storey buildings, constructed in the dark grey masonry common in northern China, and covered by heavy tiled roofs. The architects tied these old buildings together with a modern, white construction made of steel, glass, and concrete, which corresponds perfectly with the raw building stock and underlines its sensual qualities. In doing so, they simultaneously created various additional spaces as well as a covered, semi-public system of paths providing access to the individual rooms. The centre of the complex comprises a courtyard adopted from the building stock, around which all common facilities, such as the reception and foyer, the restaurant and breakfast room, are arranged. The differently sized guestrooms and flats are all brightly and tastefully designed, each having their own enclosed open area oriented towards one of the two waterbodies, surrounded by abundant greenery. In this way, nature can be experienced in full comfort.

Ort: Guojiagou/Tianjin
Architekten: Monolith Architects
Bauherr: Beijing Luoqi Cultural Tourism Development Co., Ltd
Zimmer: 16

Location: Guojiagou/Tianjin
Architects: Monolith Architects
Client: Beijing Luoqi Cultural Tourism Development Co., Ltd
Rooms: 16

Schnitt/Grundriss
Maßstab 1:750
1 Empfang/Rezeption/ Lobby
3 Hof
4 Gästezimmer
5 Gruppen-/Familien-apartment/Suite
6 Lounge/Bar/ Frühstücksraum

Section/Floor Plan
scale 1:750
1 Front desk/ Reception/Lobby
3 Courtyard
4 Guestroom
5 Group/family flat/ Suite
6 Lounge/Bar/ Breakfast room

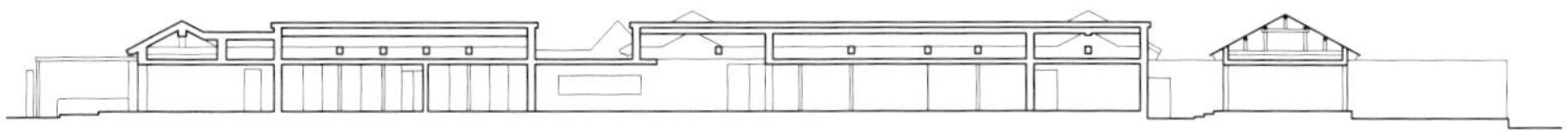

Bambus und digitale Fertigung

Bamboo and Digital Manufacture

Das Bed & Breakfast befindet sich am Rand der kleinen Ortschaft Daoming, die bekannt ist für ihre Produkte aus geflochtenen Bambusstreifen. Entstanden ist es im Zuge eines staatlich geförderten ökologischen Demonstrativbauvorhabens, das dazu beitragen soll, die überlieferte Handwerkskultur der Region wiederaufleben zu lassen, um damit die Lebenssituation auf dem Land zu verbessern. »Bamboo Craft Village« nennt sich das Projekt, das als gezielte Infrastrukturmaßnahme auch ein Besucher- sowie ein Zentrum für Handwerkskultur, eine Jugendherberge und als Krönung ein multifunktionales Gemeindehaus umfasst. Unter dessen geschwungenem Dach in Form einer Endlosschleife gibt es neben einem Restaurant und Teehaus auch Raum für Versammlungen und Seminare. Traditionelle Baustoffe wie Holz, Bambus und Ziegeldächer prägen die Architektur, die mit ihren Formen und Materialien mit der natürlichen Umgebung interagiert. Gleichzeitig versucht der Architekt Philip F. Yuan durch den Einsatz von digital gesteuerten Fertigungsprozessen ein Stück Industriekultur und technischen Fortschritt auf das Land zu bringen. Die Mehrzahl der Gästezimmer des Hotels befindet sich in dem nahe gelegen ehemaligen Bettenhaus einer Akademie. Zusätzlich dazu wurden acht frei stehende Einheiten mit ovalem Grundriss zum Übernachten am Waldrand errichtet, die in vereinfachter Form die Dachform des Gemeindezentrums aufnehmen, mit jeweils einem kleinen verglasten und begrünten Hof in der Mitte, über den die wesentliche Belichtung erfolgt. Im Inneren führen die abgerundeten Wände zu abwechslungsreich gestalteten Raumfolgen.

The bed & breakfast is located on the outskirts of the small town of Daoming, which is known for its products made of braided bamboo strips. It was created in the course of a state-funded, ecological, model building project, which is to contribute to the revival of the traditional craft culture of the region, in order to improve rural living conditions. The project, named "Bamboo Craft Village", encompasses targeted infrastructural measures, which also includes a visitor centre as well as a centre for handicraft culture, a youth hostel, and a multifunctional community building as a highlight. Underneath its curved roof shaped like an infinite loop there is a restaurant and a teahouse as well as space for meetings and seminars. Traditional materials such as timber, bamboo, and tiled roofs characterise the architecture, which interacts with the natural environment through its forms and materials. At the same time, the architect, Philip F. Yuan, endeavoured to bring a piece of industrial culture and technical progress to the countryside by applying digitally controlled manufacturing processes.
Most of the guestrooms of the hotel are located in the nearby former bedroom building of an academy. In addition, eight free-standing units with an oval floorplan were built for overnight stays at the edge of the forest, which take up the roof shape of the community centre in a simplified form, with a small, glazed, and greened courtyard each in the centre, providing the main source of lighting. Inside, the rounded walls lead to a diversely designed sequencing of rooms.

Ort: Daoming/Sichuan
Architekten: Philip F. Yuan/Archi-Union
Bauherr: Daoming Bamboo Craft Village
Zimmer: 8

Location: Daoming/Sichuan
Architects: Philip F. Yuan/Archi-Union
Client: Daoming Bamboo Craft Village
Rooms: 8

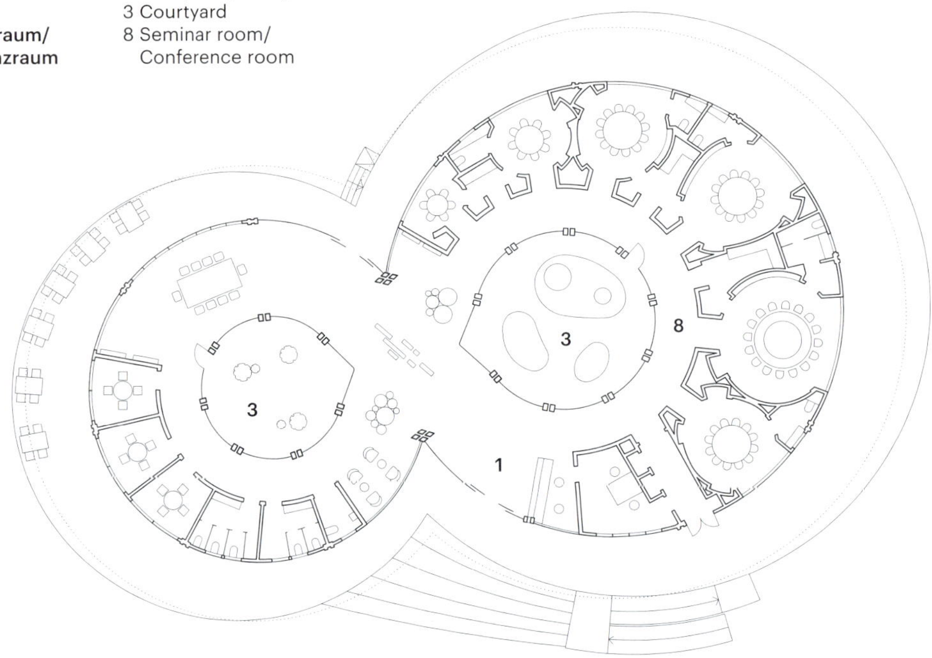

Grundriss
Maßstab 1:400
1 Empfang/Rezeption/ Lobby
3 Hof
8 Seminarraum/ Konferenzraum

Floor Plan
scale 1:400
1 Front desk/ Reception/Lobby
3 Courtyard
8 Seminar room/ Conference room

Individuelle Gestaltung, edle Ausstrahlung

Individual Design, Noble Charm

Trotz ihrer etwas abseitigen Lage auf dem Hochplateau von Yunnan gehört die uralte, geschichtsträchtige Stadt Dali mittlerweile zu den großen Touristendestinationen in China. Kein Wunder, denn neben ihrer faszinierenden Lage in einer malerischen Landschaft auf beinahe 2000 Metern Höhe am Erhai-See hat sie mit ihrer weitgehend erhaltenen Stadtmauer und deren eindrucksvollen Toren noch eine Menge weiterer Attraktionen zu bieten. Hotels aller Größenordnungen schießen dort deshalb wie Pilze aus dem Boden.
Das kleine Sunyata-Hotel mit gerade einmal 14 Zimmern befindet sich in einem dicht bebauten Gebiet in der Altstadt und ist vor allem nach innen orientiert, denn das Grundstück ermöglicht keine besonderen Ausblicke. Verteilt sind die Gästezimmer, die entsprechend dem unregelmäßigen Zuschnitt des Grundstücks alle in Größe und Form variieren, auf insgesamt acht Baukörper. Diese sind um zwei Höfe herum angeordnet, die durch einen transparenten Teepavillon räumlich getrennt werden, visuell aber verbunden bleiben. Auch das öffentlich zugängliche Café ist an seiner Ostseite zur Straße hin großflächig verglast.
Trotz der beengten Situation und der vielen Auflagen aus örtlichen Bauvorschriften, denen nicht zuletzt die geneigten Dächer geschuldet sind, gelingt es den Architekten, einen ebenso abwechslungsreich wie modern gestalteten Ort mit edler Ausstrahlung zu schaffen – ein Hotel mit hoher Aufenthaltsqualität.

In spite of its somewhat remote location on the high plateau of Yunnan, the ancient, history-charged city of Dali has in the meanwhile become one of the great tourist destinations of China. No wonder, since alongside its fascinating location in a scenic landscape, at an elevation of almost 2,000 metres and by the shores of Erhai Lake, it has many further attractions to offer, such as the largely preserved city wall and its impressive gates. Hotels of all sizes are therefore springing up like mushrooms.
The small Sunyata Hotel, with just 14 rooms, is located in a densely built-up area of the old city, and is primarily oriented inwards, since the plot doesn't offer any special views. The guestrooms, which all vary in size and shape according to the irregular cut of the plot, are spread across a total of eight buildings. These are arranged around two courtyards, which are spatially divided by a transparent tea pavilion while remaining visually connected. The publicly accessible café, too, is extensively glazed on its eastern side towards the road.
Notwithstanding the confined situation and numerous stipulations in local building regulations, which have in particular led to the sloping roofs, the architects succeeded in creating a place with a noble charm, whose design is as diverse as it is modern – a hotel with high amenity value.

Ort: Dali/Yunnan
Architekten: zhaoyang architects
Bauherr: Travelling with Hotel Management
Zimmer: 14

Location: Dali/Yunnan
Architects: Zhaoyang Architects
Client: Travelling with Hotel Management
Rooms: 14

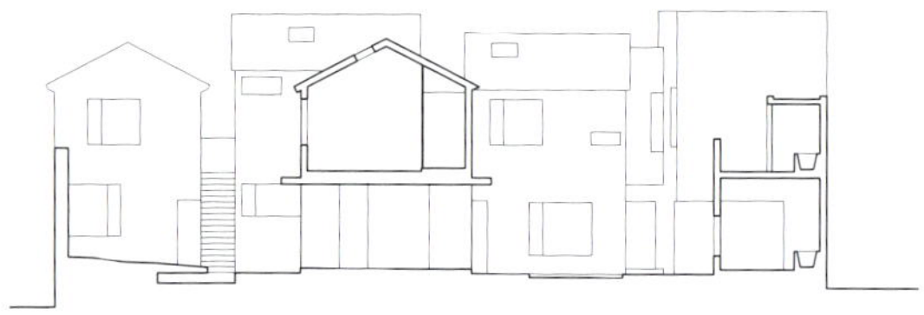

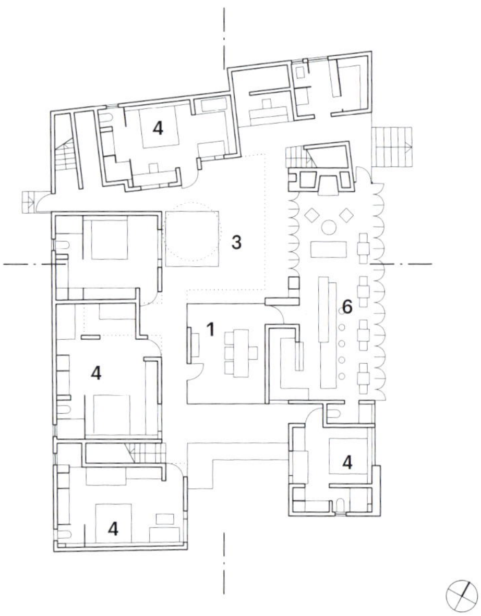
4
3
6
1
4
4
4
4

4
4
4
4
4
4
4
4
4

Schnitt/Grundrisse
Maßstab 1:400
1 Empfang/ Rezeption/Lobby
3 Hof
4 Gästezimmer
6 Lounge/ Bar/ Frühstücksraum

Section/Floor Plans
scale 1:400
1 Front desk/ Reception/Lobby
3 Courtyard
4 Guestroom
6 Lounge/Bar/Breakfast room

Übernachten zwischen Felsen

Overnight Stays in Between Rocks

China hat Tausende Kilometer Küste, und so verwundert es nicht, dass es dort auch immer häufiger gut gestaltete Gästehäuser mit Meerblick gibt. An einem weithin bekannten Strand nördlich der Hafenstadt Xiamen liegt das Nashare Hotel inmitten eines kleinen Walds aus Akazien und Kiefern. Allem voran aber wird die Landschaft hier von den runden Felsen geprägt, die wie riesige Findlinge am Ufer verstreut sind. Das Erlebnis der Natur sowie die Beziehung zur Landschaft hatten bei der Konzeption des Hotels die oberste Priorität. Acht der lediglich zwölf Zimmer sind als separate Einheiten mit jeweils eigenem Eingang und Garten in die vorhandene Topografie eingebettet, die vier anderen sind im renovierten Altbau untergebracht, wo sich auch Rezeption und Restaurant befinden. Das wirklich Besondere aber ist, wie die Felsen mit ihrer natürlichen Oberfläche direkt in die Räume und damit auch in das Design integriert sind, das von dem faszinierenden Kontrast zwischen dem rohen Stein und der modernen Ausstattung lebt. Die Felsen verleihen den Zimmern nicht nur einen ebenso ungewöhnlichen wie sinnlichen Charakter, sondern jeweils auch ein individuelles Gesicht, denn mal taucht der Fels im Bad auf, woanders im Schlafraum hinter dem Bett oder im gärtnerisch gestalteten Hof. So ist das Nashare Hotel der ideale Ort, um abseits von Hektik und Trubel zu relaxen und dabei die eindrucksvolle Szenerie zu genießen, einschließlich der Ausblicke auf den Ozean.

China has thousands of kilometres of coastline, so it is not surprising that more and more often well-designed guesthouses with sea views can be found here. At a widely known beach, north of the port city of Xiamen, the Nashare Hotel lies in the midst of a small forest of acacia and pine trees. The landscape here is, however, primarily shaped by round rocks spread across the shore like huge boulders. The experience of nature as well as the relationship with the landscape were the top priority in the hotel's conception. Eight of the only twelve rooms have been embedded into the existing topography as separate units, each with their own entrance and garden, while the four remaining rooms are housed in the renovated old building, where the reception and restaurant are also located. However, what is truly special is how the rocks, with their natural surface, have been directly integrated into the spaces and hence into the design, too, which draws on the fascinating contrast between the rough stone and the modern furnishings. The rocks not only lend the rooms a character as unusual as it is sensual but also an individual expression: sometimes, a rock has been placed in a bathroom, and elsewhere, in a bedroom behind the bed, or in the horticulturally designed courtyard. The Nashare Hotel is thus the ideal place to relax away from the hustle and bustle, while enjoying the impressive scenery and the views of the ocean.

Ort: Xiamen/Fujian
Architekten: C+ Architects, Naza Design Studio
Innenarchitekten: Deep Design Consultant
Bauherr: Naza Hotels
Zimmer: 12

Location: Xiamen/Fujian
Architects: C+ Architects, Naza Design Studio
Interior architects: Deep Design Consultant
Client: Naza Hotels
Rooms: 12

Lageplan	Site plan
Maßstab 1:750	scale 1:750
1 Empfang/Rezeption/ Lobby	1 Front desk/ Reception/Lobby
4 Gästezimmer	4 Guestroom

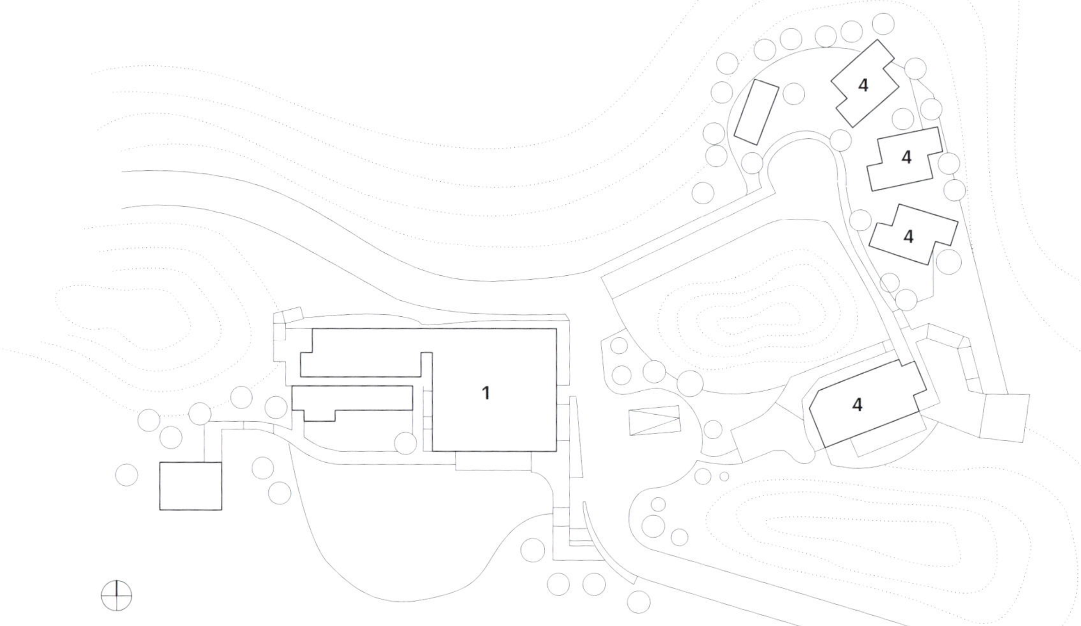

Durchgestylte Räume

Stylish Spaces

Das Hotel Wind in Xiamen ist ein typisches Design-Hotel. Gegliedert in drei Baukörper, zeigt es sich von außen als eine Anhäufung klarer, weißer Boxen am Fuße eines üppig begrünten Bergs, im Inneren als eine erlebnisreich angelegte Folge von Räumen. Das beginnt mit der Erschließung, die nicht geradlinig durch das Haus verläuft, sondern sich immer wieder aufweitet zu besonderen Orten mit Aufenthaltsqualität, zu Sitzecken, Lounges und Lesebereichen, wo Lifestyle-Magazine ausliegen und Kunst die Wände schmückt. Drei schmale, verglaste Lichthöfe, die jeweils einem anderen Motto entsprechend gestaltet sind, durchstoßen diese Zonen, verzahnen außen und innen miteinander und bringen viel Helligkeit herein.

Nicht zuletzt aber merkt man den vollkommen durchgeplanten Gästezimmern und Suiten die Lust ihrer Entwerfer an liebevoll gestalteten Ausbaudetails an. Nichts ist hier dem Zufall überlassen, von der in das Bett integrierten Nachttischbeleuchtung bis zur Wandnische für Seife und Shampoos in der Dusche. Formen und Farben sind reduziert: Der Fußboden und der untere Teil der Wände strahlt den warmen Ton von Teakholz aus, der Rest der Flächen ist von klarem Weiß geprägt, das dann in dem zum Raum hin offenen Bad in das dezente Grau von Sichtbeton und örtlichem Granit übergeht.

Die Krönung des Hotels jedoch ist das Restaurant auf dem Dach, durch dessen großflächig verglaste Fassaden sich der Blick auf den Berg und das Meer öffnet. Schade nur, dass trotz etwas abseitiger Lage die Umgebung doch ziemlich verbaut ist.

The Hotel Wind in Xiamen is a typical design hotel. From the outside, it appears as an aggregation of three of clear, white boxes at the foot of a lushly green mountain from the outside, and from the inside as an eventfully arranged sequence of spaces. It starts with the circulation, which doesn't run through the building in a linear fashion but repeatedly widens into special locations with lounging qualities, such as seating areas, lounges, and reading areas, where lifestyle magazines are available and art adorns the walls. Three narrow, glazed atriums, each designed according to a different motto, pierce these zones and interlock the outside with the inside, while letting in a lot of light.

The meticulously planned out guestrooms and suites evince their designers' delight in lovingly designed finishing details. Nothing has been left to chance here – from the bedside table lighting integrated into the bed to the wall niche for soap and shampoo in the shower. Shapes and colours are restrained: the floor and the lower part of the walls exude the warm tone of teak wood, while the remaining surfaces are characterised by clear white, which then merges into the understated grey colour of the exposed concrete and the local granite of the bathroom, which opens towards the room.

The highlight of the hotel, however, is the rooftop restaurant, whose extensively glazed facades permit views of the mountain and the sea. It's just a pity that, in spite of the somewhat remote location, the surroundings are rather built up.

Ort: Xiamen/Fujian
Architekten: Team_BLDG
Zimmer: 37

Location: Xiamen/Fujian
Architects: Team_BLDG
Rooms: 37

Grundrisse
Maßstab 1:750
1 Empfang/Rezeption/ Lobby
4 Gästezimmer

Floor Plans
scale 1:750
1 Front desk/ Reception/Lobby
4 Guestroom

Ein Hofhaus als Design-Hotel

A Courtyard House as a Design Hotel

Wer die einzigartige Atmosphäre eines traditionellen Hofhauses in Beijing erleben will, ist im sth.here genau am richtigen Ort. Das privat betriebene und mit nur sechs Gästezimmern ausgesprochen kleine Boutique-Hotel befindet sich im White Pagoda Temple Hutong nahe dem Beihai-Park im Zentrum der Stadt in einem der wenigen noch verbliebenen ursprünglichen Wohnquartiere.

Äußerlich zeigt nur der modern gestaltete Eingang zwischen dem üblichen grauen Mauerwerk die neue Nutzung an. Vorbei an dem kleinen Café und Frühstücksraum gelangt der Reisende von dort in den Hof, der die einzelnen Zimmer erschließt. Jedes davon ist individuell und mit liebevollen Einrichtungsdetails gestaltet, und jedes offenbart ein eigenes Raumkonzept, das seinen besonderen Charme ausmacht. In einigen ist das Bett auf einer Galerie unter dem Dach angeordnet, in anderen orientiert sich der Schlafplatz hin zu einem schmalen, teilweise begrünten Lichthof. In Zimmer 1 ist der Lichthof oben verglast und bleibt zum Schlafbereich und zum grau gehaltenen Bad hin offen. Der Vorraum mit Garderobe und Schreibtisch ist zum Hof hin großflächig transparent ausgebildet. Bei geöffneter Jalousie entsteht ein visueller Kontakt nach außen – der zur Straße abgeschlossene halböffentliche Erschließungsraum dient der Begegnung und Kommunikation. Oder man trifft sich auf der kleinen Dachterrasse unter dem großen, schattenspendenden Baum. Hier oben hört man die Vögel zwitschern und fühlt sich der hektischen Großstadt entrückt. Und abends bei einem Glas Wein, wenn im Hutong langsam die Lichter ausgehen, ist der Besucher überrascht, wie ruhig es im Zentrum einer der größten Metropolen doch sein kann.

For those wishing to experience the unique atmosphere of a traditional courtyard house in Beijing, the sth.here is just the right place to do so. The privately run and notably small boutique hotel, with only six guestrooms, is located in the White Pagoda Temple Hutong near the Beihai Park in the city centre, in one of the few remaining original residential quarters.
On the outside, only the modern design of the entrance in between the usual grey masonry indicates a new use. Passing the small café and breakfast room, travellers reach the courtyard from there, which provides access to the individual rooms. Each room has been individually designed, including lovely furnishing details, and reveals its own spatial concept, exuding a special charm. In some rooms, the bed is arranged on a raised platform underneath the roof, while in others, the sleeping area is oriented towards a narrow, partly greened atrium. In room 1, the atrium is glazed at the top and remains open towards the sleeping area and the grey bathroom. The anteroom, with a cloakroom and a desk, is extensively transparent towards the courtyard. When the blinds are open, a visual link to the outside is created – the semi-public access room, closed off towards the road, serves as a meeting and communication space. Alternatively, one can meet people on the small roof terrace beneath the large, shady tree. Up here, one hears the birds chirping and feels removed from the hectic metropolis; and in the evenings, over a glass of wine, when the lights slowly go out in the Hutong, visitors are surprised how quiet it can be in the centre of one of the largest metropolises.

Ort: Beijing
Architekten: B.L.U.E. Architecture Studio
Bauherr: privat
Zimmer: 6

Location: Beijing
Architects: B.L.U.E. Architecture Studio
Client: private
Rooms: 6

Grundriss	Floor Plan
Maßstab 1:400	scale 1:400
1 Eingang	1 Reception
3 Hof	3 Courtyard
4 Gästezimmer	4 Guestroom
6 Frühstücksraum	6 Breakfast room
9 Galerie	9 Gallery

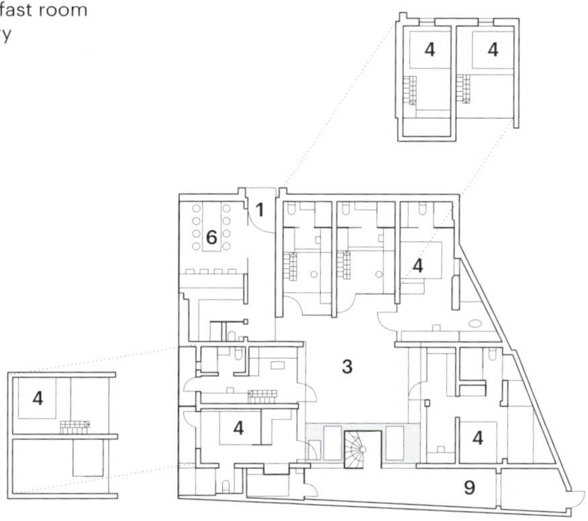

Ein vielschichtiger Hof

A Multilayered Courtyard

Hutel, was so viel heißen soll wie Hutong Hotel, nennt sich das kleine, aber noble Gästehaus, das sich in einer ehemaligen Bäckerei in einem der traditionellen Hofhausquartiere nahe dem Qianmen-Tor im Zentrum von Beijing verbirgt. Von außen verrät kaum etwas die neue Nutzung. Hat der Gast aber erst die rote Tür in der klassisch grauen Ziegelwand mit ihren Rundbogenfenstern durchschritten, findet er sich unversehens in einem modernen Ambiente mit viel Glas. Alle Trennwände im halböffentlichen Bereich des Hotels sind transparent, mit begrünten Lichthöfen zwischen den Räumen. Auch vor den Gästezimmern im Erdgeschoss liegen solche Höfe, um diesen Privatheit zu geben.
Daher fällt auch vom Bett der Blick direkt in einen verglasten Lichthof, der in spannungsvollem Kontrast steht zu dem mit viel Holz ausgekleideten Raum und dennoch mit seiner edlen Gestaltung und seiner Bepflanzung mit Bambus perfekt mit diesem korrespondiert. Überall im Haus beziehen die – trotz beengter Situation – sehr hellen Zimmer ihren besonderen Charme aus dem gelungenen Zusammenspiel von Alt und Neu. Das gilt auch für den lichtdurchfluteten Speiseraum, wo sich die Gäste an einer langen Tafel unter einem großen traditionellen Holzdach zum Frühstück treffen. Abgeschottet von dicken Mauern, ist das im Inneren offene Haus mit seinen sieben Gästezimmern eine Oase der Ruhe inmitten eines quirligen Stadtviertels.

Ort: Beijing
Architekten: Archstudio
Bauherr: Hutel
Zimmer: 7

Hutel, short for Hutong Hotel, is the name of the small but noble guesthouse tucked away in a former bakery in one of the traditional courtyard house quarters close to the Qianmen Gate in the centre of Beijing. From the outside, hardly anything suggests its new use. Once guests have passed through the red door in the classic grey brick wall with its arched windows, however, they unexpectedly find themselves in a modern ambience with extensive glazing. All dividing walls in the semi-public area of the hotel are transparent, with greened atriums between the spaces. Such courtyards are also located in front of the guestrooms on the ground floor, lending them privacy.
The view from the bed is therefore also of a glazed atrium, which stands in suspenseful contrast to the room with its abundant wooden cladding, while its refined design and bamboo planting corresponds perfectly. Throughout the building, the very bright rooms, despite the confined situation, derive their special charm from the successful interplay between the old and the new. This also applies to the dining room, bathed in light, where the guests meet for breakfast at a long table underneath a large, traditional timber roof. Sealed off by thick walls, the building – open on the inside and with its seven guestrooms – is an oasis of calm in the midst of a lively district.

Location: Beijing
Architects: Archstudio
Client: Hutel
Rooms: 7

Schnitt/Grundriss
Maßstab 1:400
1 Rezeption
2 Restaurant
3 Lichthof
4 Gästezimmer
6 Frühstücksraum
7 Küche
12 Personal

Section/Floor Plan
scale 1:400
1 Reception
2 Restaurant
3 Courtyard
4 Guestroom
6 Breakfast room
7 Kitchen
12 Staff

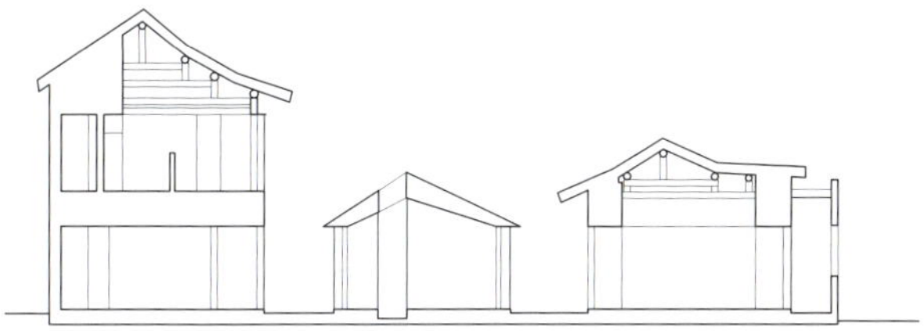

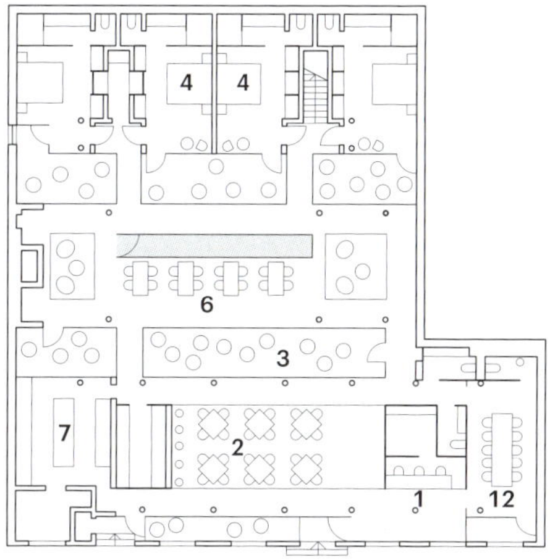

Labyrinth aus Höfen

A Labyrinth of Courtyards

Wegen seiner markanten Mauern wird das Tsingpu Yangzhou Retreat auch The Walled genannt. Nicht weit entfernt von Yangzhous größter Attraktion, dem Slender West Lake, liegt es in einem Gebiet, das überzogen ist von unzähligen kleinen künstlichen Seen. Einige davon befinden sich auf dem Grundstück und sind ebenso in die Anlage integriert wie verschiedene weniger bedeutende Bestandsbauten. Um diese gestalterisch mit den Neubauten zusammenzubinden, entschieden sich die Architekten Lyndon Neri und Rossana Hu für ein Raster aus grauen Ziegelmauern, die dem Komplex nun seinen unverwechselbaren Charakter geben. Gleichzeitig schaffen sie damit, anknüpfend an die chinesische Bautradition, eine spannungsvolle Abfolge von Höfen unterschiedlicher Größe und Qualität. Diese vermitteln zwischen Innen- und Außenraum, verbinden die Landschaft mit der Architektur und rahmen den Blick, zum Himmel ebenso wie auf den Boden. Die meisten der Gästezimmer gleichermaßen zu einzelnen Freibereichen orientieren sich, ebenso wie die gemeinschaftlichen Einrichtungen von der Rezeption über das Restaurant bis zur Bibliothek. Andere Freiflächen sind als abstrakte Gärten gestaltet und eignen sich hervorragend zum Relaxen. Gemeinsames Merkmal all dieser Höfe ist das sinnlich raue Mauerwerk aus recycelten Steinen, das der Architektur ihre besondere Anmutung verleiht. Wie von Neri&Hu nicht anders zu erwarten, ist auch die Inneneinrichtung edel gestaltet: The Walled ist ein Luxusresort aus einem Guss, bestens geeignet für Design-Enthusiasten.

Thanks to its distinctive walls, the Tsingpu Yangzhou Retreat is also called The Walled. Not far from Yangzhou's greatest attraction, the Slender West Lake, it lies in an area specked with innumerable small artificial lakes. Some of them are located on the plot and integrated into the complex, just as various more minor existing buildings. To tie these in with the new buildings, the architects Lyndon Neri and Rossana Hu selected a grid of grey brick walls, which now lend the complex its distinct character. In doing so, and taking up Chinese architectural tradition, they simultaneously created a suspenseful sequence of courtyards of various sizes and qualities. These mediate between indoor and outdoor spaces, while linking the landscape with the architecture and framing the views of both the sky and the ground. Most guestrooms are likewise oriented towards the individual open areas, as are the common facilities, from the reception to the restaurant to the library. Other open spaces have been designed as abstract gardens and are excellently suited for relaxing. The common feature of all these courtyards is the sensuously raw masonry of recycled stones, which gives the architecture its special charm. As can be expected from Neri&Hu, the interiors are also exquisitely designed: The Walled is a completely rounded luxury resort, eminently suitable for design enthusiasts.

Ort: Yangzhou/Jiangsu
Architekten: Neri&Hu Design and Research Office
Bauherr: Shi Huijuan
Zimmer: 20

Location: Yangzhou/Jiangsu
Architects: Neri&Hu Design and Research Office
Client: Shi Huijuan
Rooms: 20

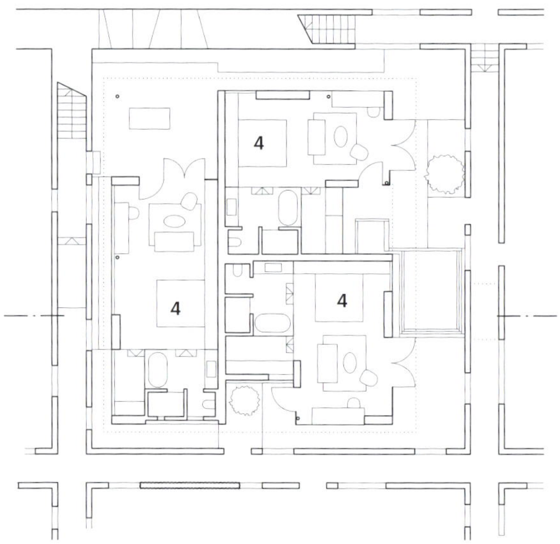
4
4
4

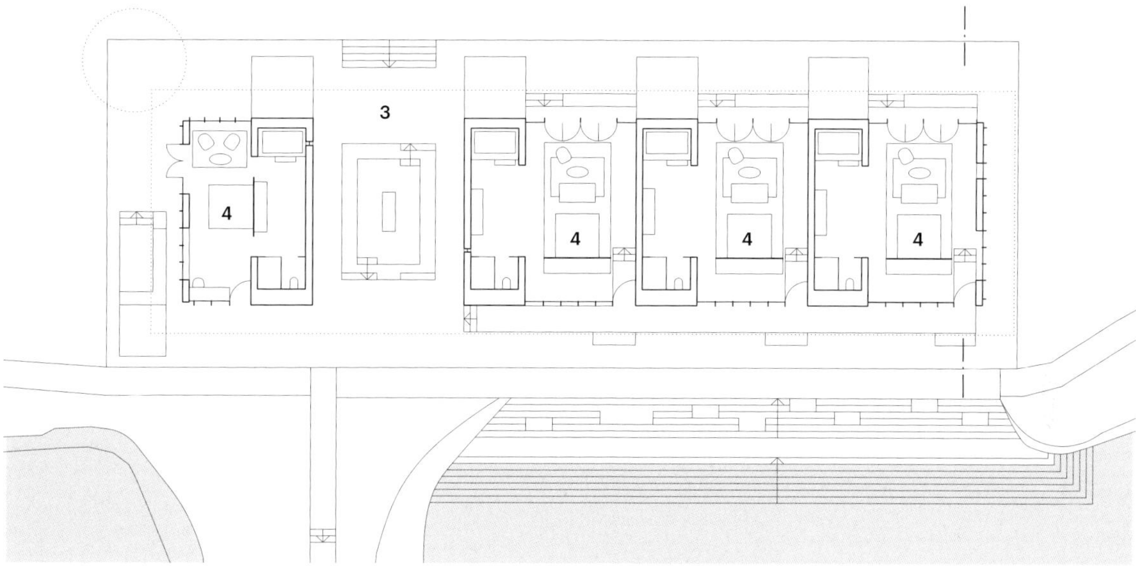

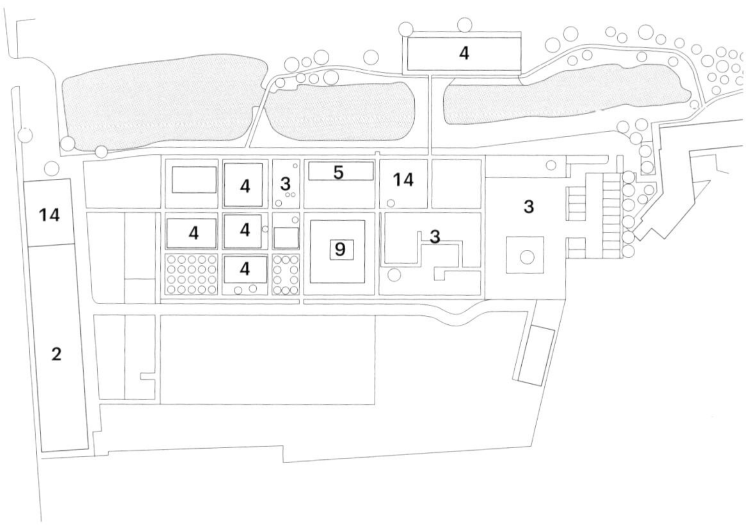

Übersichtsplan
Maßstab 1:2500
Grundrisse – Ausschnitte
Maßstab 1:400
2 Restaurant
3 Hof
4 Gästezimmer
5 Gruppen-/Familien-apartment/Suite
9 Bibliothek/Galerie
14 Bühne

Plan Overview
scale 1:2,500
Floor Plans – extracts
scale 1:400
2 Restaurant
3 Courtyard
4 Guestroom
5 Group/family flat/Suite
9 Library/Gallery
14 Stage

Ein inszeniertes Lagerhaus

A Choreographed Warehouse

Rußspuren an den Wänden, Löcher im Putz und Reste billiger Fliesen als Hintergrund in einer gestylten Nobelherberge – mit seinem radikalen Konzept ist The Waterhouse längst zu einem Klassiker unter den Design-Hotels in China avanciert. Mit der regelrechten Inszenierung eines vormals eher unbedeutenden Lagergebäudes ist es zur Zeit seiner Eröffnung 2010 eines der ersten international beachteten Projekte, das eine Trendwende im Land signalisiert: die Wiederentdeckung des Bestands. Denn was die Architekten Lyndon Neri und Rossana Hu in der ehemaligen Hafengegend am South Bund in Shanghai so spektakulär umgestalten, wäre nur wenige Jahre vorher noch gnadenlos der Abrissbirne zum Opfer gefallen und durch einen Neubau ersetzt worden. Besonders faszinierend wirkt das Zusammenspiel von ruppigen Oberflächen des Altbaus und edlen Einbauten in der hohen Eingangshalle sowie in dem angrenzenden Restaurant und Barbereich, wo die Gäste nun zwischen bröckelnden Betonstützen und rostigem Stahl ihr Dinner genießen. Die Zimmer selbst sind vielfältig und erlebnisreich gestaltet. Großflächige Verglasungen, die aber mit Vorhängen geschlossen werden können, ermöglichen die Durchsicht in den Erschließungsbereich oder zum Nachbarn und sorgen für ein besonderes Raumerlebnis. The Waterhouse ist ein Hotel mit urbanem Flair und teilweise eindrucksvollen Ausblicken auf die Skyline von Pudong, das neben dem rauen Charme eines alten Industriebaus zugleich Luxus und Komfort bietet.

Traces of soot on the walls, holes in the plaster, and remnants of cheap tiles as backdrop for a stylish and plush hotel: with its radical concept, The Waterhouse has long since become a classic among the design hotels in China. A downright orchestration of a former rather insignificant warehouse, it became one of the first internationally noted projects signalising a turning point in the country when it opened in 2010, namely the rediscovery of the existing stock. What the architects Lyndon Neri and Rossana Hu so spectacularly redesigned in the former port area at the South Bund in Shanghai, would only a few years earlier have mercilessly fallen victim to the demolition ball and been replaced by a new building. Particularly fascinating is the interplay between the rough surfaces in the old building and the exquisite furnishings in the high entrance hall as well as the adjoining restaurant and bar area, where guests can now enjoy their dinner amidst a backdrop of crumbling concrete columns and rusted steel. The rooms themselves are designed in a diverse and eventful manner. Extensive glazing, which can, however, be covered by curtains, allows for views of the circulation area or towards the neighbours, and provides a special spatial experience. The Waterhouse is a hotel with urban flair and partly impressive views of the skyline of Pudong, simultaneously offering both the raw charm of an old industrial building as well as luxury and comfort.

Ort: Shanghai
Architekten: Neri&Hu Design and Research Office
Bauherr: Cameron Holdings Hotel Management Ltd.
Zimmer: 19

Location: Shanghai
Architects: Neri&Hu Design and Research Office
Client: Cameron Holdings Hotel Management Ltd.
Rooms: 19

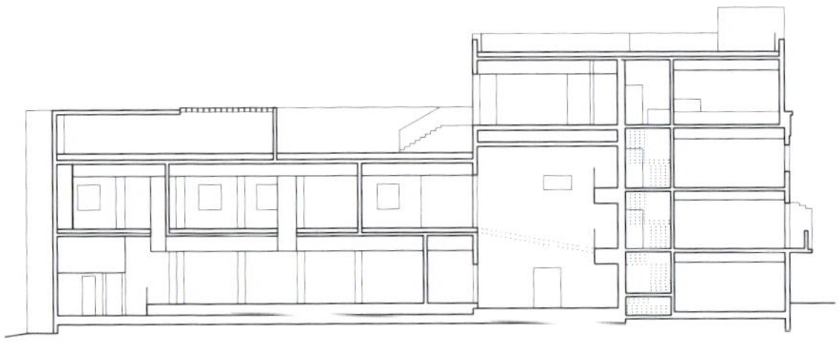

Schnitte/Grundrisse
Maßstab 1:750
1 Rezeption/Lobby
2 Restaurant
3 Hof
4 Gästezimmer
6 Bar/Frühstücksraum
7 Küche

Sections/Floor Plans
scale 1:750
1 Reception/Lobby
2 Restaurant
3 Courtyard
4 Guestroom
6 Bar/Breakfast room
7 Kitchen

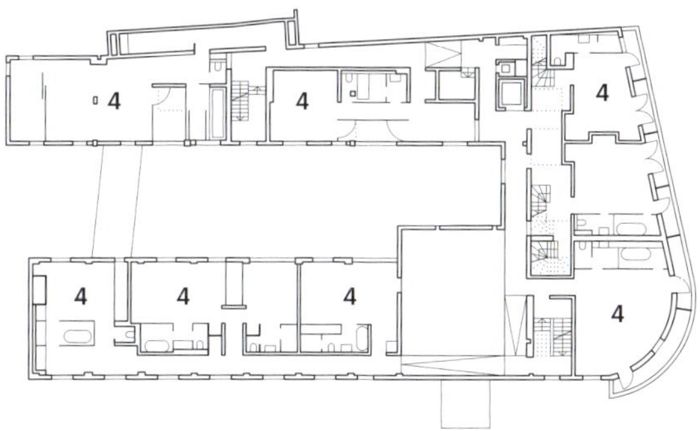
4
4
4
4
4
4
4
4

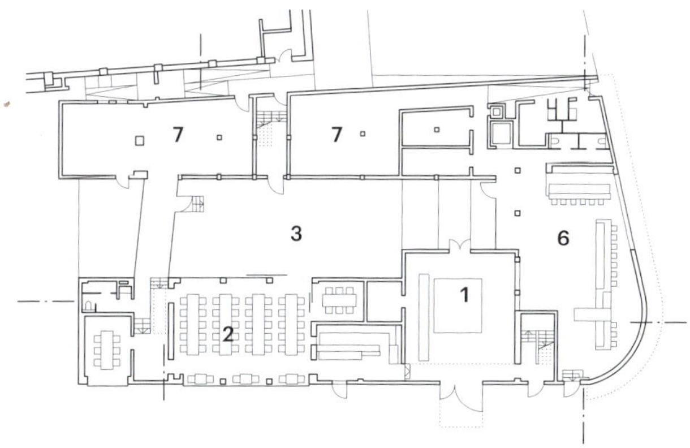
7
7
3
6
1
2

Hofhaus auf dem Dach

A Rooftop Courtyard House

Ein strahlend weißer Zylinder mit einer Haut aus perforiertem Metall verrät von außen die besondere Nutzung in dem ansonsten eher grauen Vorort der Megametropole Shanghai. Doch niemand würde hinter der niedrigeren Bebauung am Straßenrand den komplex gestalteten Garten erwarten, der den Bau umgibt.
In den unteren beiden Geschossen des runden ehemaligen Vertriebsgebäudes hat sich der frühere Manager einer Fabrik für Emaille-Waren ein kleines Museum eingerichtet, um seine Sammlung zu diesem Thema auszustellen. Sein Sohn, in derselben Branche tätig, belegt mit dem eigenen Unternehmen den zweiten Stock. Die eigentliche Überraschung aber ist das kleine Bed & Breakfast in der Aufstockung darüber, das heute überwiegend für Gäste der Firma genutzt wird. Unvermittelt findet sich der Besucher in einem traditionell anmutenden chinesischen Hof, über den er sein Zimmer erreicht. Sobald er dieses betritt, ändert sich der Eindruck und der Blick fällt auf den ausgesprochen modern gestalteten und mit Bambus und Bonsais begrünten Balkon, der als »Freibereich in der Luft« hinter der transluzenten Aluminiumhülle liegt, die die verschiedenen Geschosse des Rundbaus zusammenbindet. Der Architekt Yu Ting, ein Verfechter der Philosophie von These und Antithese, inszeniert hier geschickt den Kontrast zwischen dem Überlieferten und dem Zeitgemäßen, dem rechteckigen Hof und der zylindrischen Gebäudeform, dem üppigen Garten außen und den klaren Formen im Inneren. Die Zimmer selbst sind angenehm klar gestaltet, mit einigen bewussten Akzenten aus Holz und sorgfältig ausgewählten Accessoires. Leider liegt die Unterkunft aber etwas weit vom pulsierenden Zentrum der Stadt entfernt.

A shining white cylinder, with a skin of perforated metal, reveals its special use from the outside in this otherwise rather grey suburb of the megacity of Shanghai. However, nobody would expect a complexly designed garden surrounds the building behind the low-rise development along the roadside. On the two lower floors of the circular, former sales and marketing building, the erstwhile manager of a factory for enamel wares has installed a small museum, to exhibit his collection on this topic. His son, who works in the same field, occupies the second floor with his own company. The actual surprise, however, is the small bed and breakfast in the extension above it, which is today mostly used for guests of the company. Unexpectedly, visitors find themselves in a traditional-looking Chinese courtyard. From here, they enter their rooms and the impression changes: The distinctly modern design of the balcony, greened with bamboo and bonsai, forming an "open area in the air" behind a translucent aluminium shell, ties together the different floors of the circular building. Here, the architect Yu Ting, an advocate of the philosophy of thesis and antithesis, skilfully orchestrates the contrast between what has been passed down and the contemporary; the rectangular courtyard and the cylindrical building shape; the lush garden outside and the clear forms inside. The rooms themselves have been designed in a pleasantly clear-cut manner, with some deliberate accents of wood and carefully selected accessories. Unfortunately, the accommodation is somewhat far from the pulsating city centre.

Ort: Shanghai
Architekten: Yu Ting/Wutopia Lab
Bauherr: Shi Huijuan
Zimmer: 5

Location: Shanghai
Architects: Yu Ting/Wutopia Lab
Client: Shi Huijuan
Rooms: 5

Schnitt/Grundriss
Maßstab 1:400
1 Zugang
3 Innenhof
4 Gästezimmer
6 Lounge/Frühstücksraum
13 Terrasse

Section/Floor Plan
scale 1:400
1 Entrance
3 Courtyard
4 Guestroom
6 Lounge/Breakfast room
13 Terrace

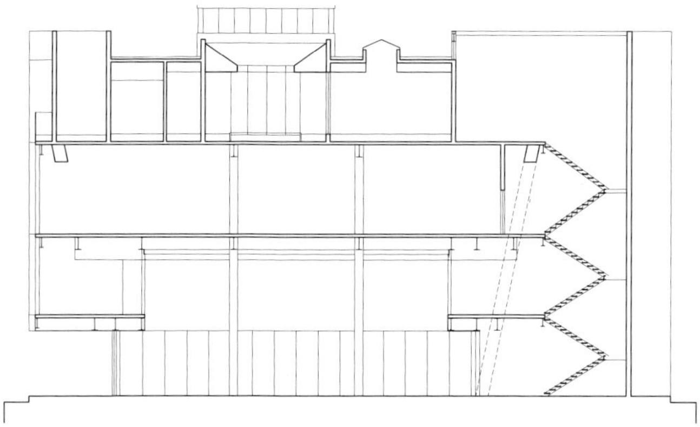

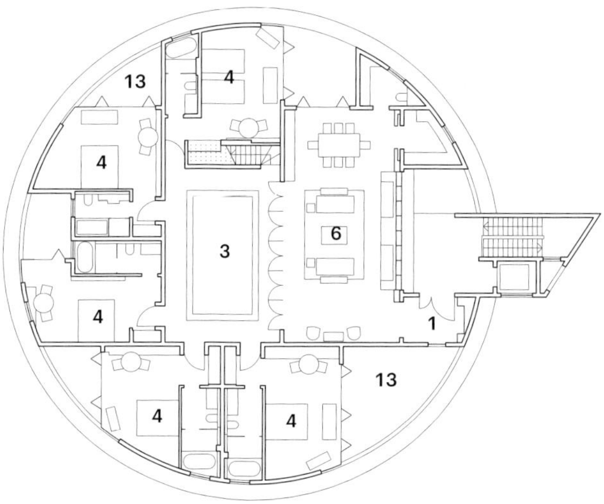

Betonskulptur als Hostel

A Concrete Sculpture as Hostel

Skulptural angeordnete Betonkuben in einem engen Hof, jeder an seiner Front verglast und im Inneren durch eine Luke erschlossen, dienen als Schlafkojen, in einem weiteren Kubus befinden sich Dusche und WC – der Micro Hutong versteht sich mehr als Konzeptstudie denn als ein mit einer konkreten Funktion belegtes Gebäude. Nach Vorstellungen seines Architekten Zhang Ke kann er als Hostel für Kinder ebenso genutzt werden wie als Mini-Sozialwohnung oder als temporäres Refugium für einen Künstler. Der dazugehörige große Raum im Altbau an der Straße fungiert dann als Gemeinschaftraum oder in letzterem Fall als Werkstatt und Ausstellungsbereich. Gleichzeitig vermittelt er zwischen den privaten Rückzugsbereichen und dem städtischen Gefüge außenherum.
Hutongs mit ihren an enge Gassen angrenzenden Hofhäusern erstreckten sich als traditionelle Wohnform in Beijing ursprünglich über einen Großteil der Stadt, fielen dann aber überwiegend einer gnadenlosen Modernisierungswelle zum Opfer. Auch wenn in allerjüngster Zeit ein Umdenken stattfindet, gilt es doch Lösungen zu finden, um die wenigen verbliebenen Bauten mit neuem Leben zu füllen und damit für die Zukunft zu erhalten. Zhang Ke will mit seinen verschiedenen selbst initiierten Hutong-Projekten zeigen, was dabei außer den üblichen Souvenirshops oder Fastfood-Lokalen für Touristen möglich ist. Mit dem Micro Hutong liefert er einen ebenso ungewöhnlichen wie radikal einfachen und faszinierenden Denkanstoß.

Ort: Beijing
Architekten: ZAO/standardarchitecture
Zimmer: 5

Sculpturally arranged concrete cubes in a narrow courtyard, each glazed on the front and accessed on the inside by a hatch, serve as sleeping bunks, while another cube houses a shower and a WC – the Micro Hutong is more of a concept study than a building with a specific function. According to the conception of its architect, Zhang Ke, it can likewise be used as a hostel for children, a mini social housing flat or as a temporary retreat for an artist. The accompanying large space in the old building along the road can then function as a common room, or in the latter case, as a workshop and an exhibition area. At the same time, it mediates between the private retreat areas and the urban fabric outside.
Hutongs, as a traditional form of housing, with their courtyard houses bordering on narrow lanes, originally extended across a large part of the city but then largely fell victim to a merciless modernisation wave. Even though a rethink has been taking place in most recent times, solutions must be found to fill the few remaining buildings with new life and thus preserve them for the future. With his various self-initiated Hutong projects, Zhang Ke wants to show what is possible other than the usual souvenir shops or fast food restaurants for tourists. With the Micro Hutong, he provides a thought-provoking impulse which is as unusual as it is radically simple and fascinating.

Location: Beijing
Architects: ZAO/standardarchitecture
Rooms: 5

Schnitt/Grundrisse
Maßstab 1:400
4 Gästezimmer
6 Lounge

Section/Floor Plans
scale 1:400
4 Guestroom
6 Lounge

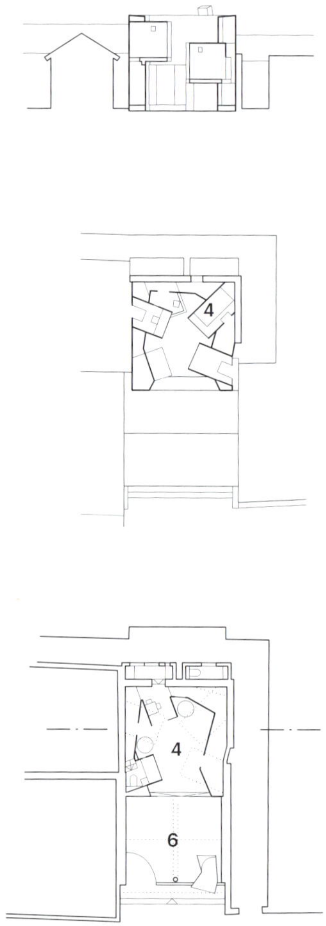

Jugendhotel mit farbigen Akzenten

Youth Hostel with Colourful Accents

Schon die Fassade macht neugierig. Scharf geschnittene Erkerfenster aus schwarz lackiertem Stahl sowie farbigen Gläser im Erdgeschoss stehen in gelungenem Kontrast zu dem ruppigen Beton des Bestands. Die Architekten von o-Office aus Guangzhou, bekannt für ihre kreativen Sanierungen, haben das ehemalige Arbeiterwohnheim einer Fabrik in Shenzhen in ein schickes Jugendhotel umgebaut, aufgrund des schmalen Budgets mit nur wenigen, dafür aber effektvollen Eingriffen. So bleibt der Charakter des Altbaus weitgehend bewahrt und auch sein Grundriss konnte überwiegend erhalten werden. Nur im Erdgeschoss finden sich anstelle der ehemaligen Schlafsäle jetzt größere Räume für die öffentlichen Funktionen der Herberge wie die Rezeption, Gemeinschaftsräume, die allgemein zugängliche Küche, eine Bar sowie ein kleines Café. Durch die kolorierten Glasfenster bietet sich aus diesen Bereichen nun ein »bunter« Blick auf die Außenwelt. Gleichermaßen sind auch die langen, geraden Flure der Bettengeschosse mit farbigem Glas aufgelockert. Die zurückhaltend einfach ausgestatteten Zimmer bekommen ihren besonderen Akzent durch die neu geschaffenen Erkernischen, die als räumlicher Übergang zwischen außen und innen zum Verweilen einladen und dabei eine Aussicht auf den umgebenden Grünraum bieten.

Already the facade excites one's curiosity. Clear-cut bay windows of black-painted steel and coloured glass on the ground floor nicely contrast with the rough concrete of the building stock. The architects from O-office in Guangzhou, known for their creative renovations, have converted the former workers' hostel of a factory in Shenzhen into a stylish youth hostel, applying only a few but effective interventions in view of a tight budget. In doing so, the character of the old building has been extensively preserved, while its floor plan, too, could largely be retained. It is only on the ground floor that, instead of the former dormitories, there now are larger spaces for the public functions of the hostel, such as the reception, common rooms, the generally accessible kitchen, a bar, as well as a small café. The coloured, glazed windows in these areas now offer a "colourful" view of the outside world. Likewise, the long, straight corridors of the bedroom floors, too, have been loosened up by coloured glass. The rooms, with their reservedly simple features, are specially accented by the newly created bay recesses, serving as spatial transition between the outside and the inside, and as an invitation to linger, while providing a view of the surrounding green space.

Ort: Shenzhen
Architekten: O-office
Bauherr: Youth Hostel of iD Town
Zimmer: 45

Location: Shenzhen
Architects: O-office
Client: Youth Hostel of iD Town
Rooms: 45

Schnitt/Grundrisse
Maßstab 1:400
1 Empfang/Rezeption/ Lobby
2 Restaurant
4 Gästezimmer
5 Gruppen-/ Familien-apartment/Suite
6 Lounge/ Bar/ Frühstücksraum
8 Seminarraum/ Konferenzraum

Section/Floor Plans
scale 1:400
1 Front desk/ Reception/Lobby
2 Restaurant
4 Guestroom
5 Group/family flat/ Suite
6 Lounge/Bar/Break-fast room
8 Seminar room/Con-ference room

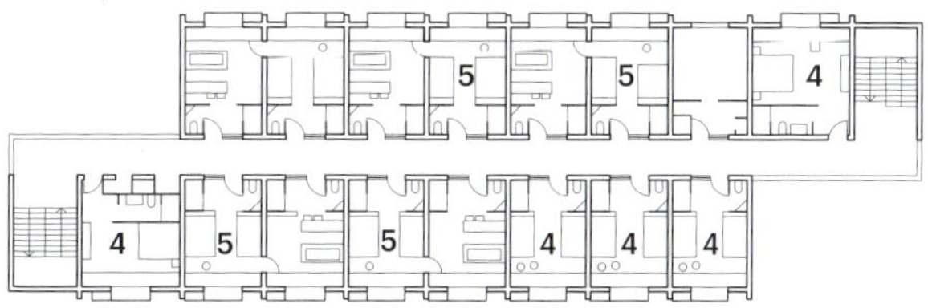

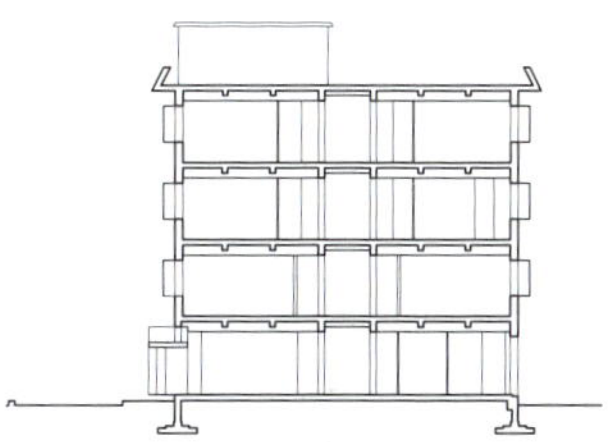

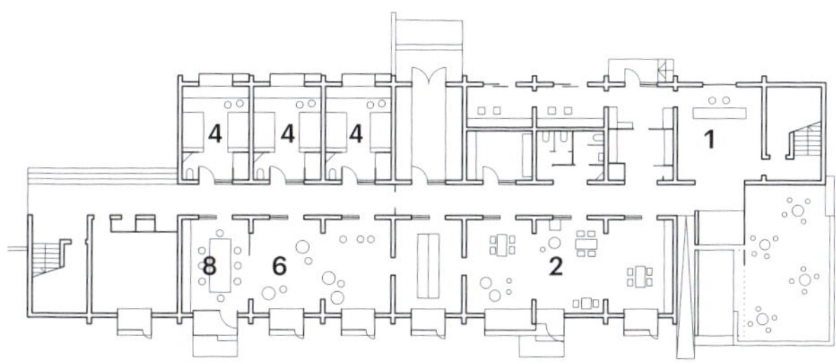

Ein Hotel als künstliche Landschaft

A Hotel as Artificial Landscape

Mit der Realisierung des Wa Shan Guest House erhielt Wang Shu, der schon den kompletten Campus der Kunstakademie in Hangzhou mit seinen 21 Einzelbauten entworfen hatte, die Gelegenheit, diesem einige Jahre nach Fertigstellung einen weiteren Baustein hinzuzufügen. Diesen nutzt er wie bislang kein anderes seiner Gebäude dazu, seine Architekturphilosophie zu demonstrieren. Analog zur Gesamtanlage gestaltet er auch das Hotel als künstliche Landschaft und fasst die verschiedenen Funktionen unter einem 120 Meter langen, mehrfach gefalteten Dach zusammen, das einem konstruierten Gebirge gleicht und mit dem natürlichen Terrain harmoniert – Wa Shan bedeutet »Berg aus Dachziegeln«. Die Tour durch das Haus bietet auf einem der drei in Längsrichtung verlaufenden Wege eine Abfolge an räumlichen Erlebnissen und ständig wechselnden Situation und Materialien. Beim Gang vom Zimmertrakt zum Restaurant oder vom Konferenzbereich zum Teehaus passiert der Besucher dicht begrünte Freibereiche, überquert auf einer Brücke ein Wasserbassin oder findet sich unvermittelt vor einer Maueröffnung, die einen spektakulären Blick auf den angrenzenden Fluss ermöglicht. Nicht zuletzt führt einer der Wege über das mit recycelten Ziegeln gedeckte Dach. So vielfältig sich die Architektur gibt, die Gästezimmer sind eher zurückhaltend und solide gestaltet. Der Bezug zur chinesischen Tradition steht auch hier im Vordergrund; das zeigt sich an einzelnen Möbelstücken, aber auch an Elementen wie der Unterdecke aus geflochtenen Bambusstreifen oder den Sonnenschutzelementen aus dem gleichen Material. Das Spazierengehen im Haus steht hier über dem Verweilen im Zimmer.

With the realisation of the Wa Shan Guesthouse, Wang Shu, who had already designed the entire campus of the China Academy of Art in Hangzhou, with its 21 individual buildings, was given the opportunity, a few years after its completion, to add to it a further component, demonstrating his architectural philosophy as clearly as perhaps in no other building to date. Like the entire complex, he designed the hotel as an artificial landscape, too, pooling the different functions beneath a 120-metre-long, repeatedly folded roof, which resembles a constructed mountain and harmonises with the natural terrain – Wa Shan means "mountain of roof tiles". A tour of the building, along one of the three longitudinal paths, offers a sequence of spatial experiences and continually changing situations and materials. When walking from the room wing to the restaurant, or from the conference area to the teahouse, visitors pass densely greened open areas, crossing a bridge above a water basin or unexpectedly finding themselves in front of an opening in a wall, which offers a spectacular view of the adjacent river. One of the paths even leads across the roof covered with recycled tiles. As diverse as the architecture is, the guestrooms are designed in a more reserved and sober manner. Again, there is a heavy focus on Chinese tradition; this can be seen in individual pieces of furniture but also in elements such as the suspended ceiling made of interwoven bamboo strips or the sun protection elements of the same material. Here, going for a walk in the building can take precedence over spending time in the room.

Ort: Hangzhou
Architekten: Wang Shu, Lu Wenyu/Amateur Architecture Studio
Bauherr: China Academy of Art
Zimmer: 30

Location: Hangzhou
Architects: Wang Shu, Lu Wenyu/Amateur Architecture Studio
Client: China Academy of Art
Rooms: 30

Schnitte/Grundrisse
Maßstab 1:1000
2 Restaurant
3 Hof
4 Gästezimmer
6 Frühstücksraum
8 Konferenzraum/ Vortragsraum
14 Bühne
15 Shop

Sections/Floor Plans
scale 1:1,000
2 Restaurant
3 Courtyard
4 Guestroom
6 Breakfast room
8 Seminar room/ Conference room
14 Stage
15 Shop

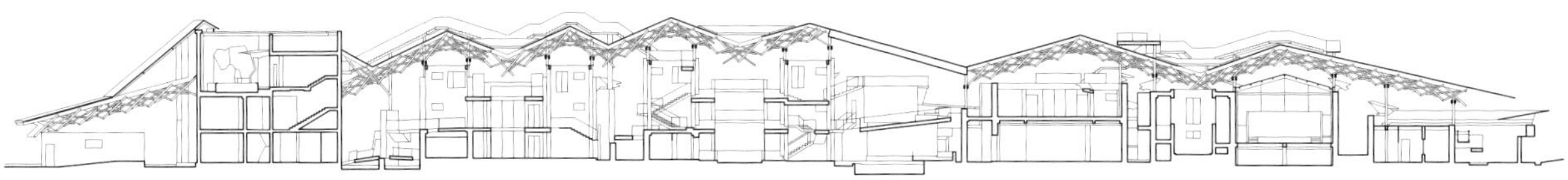

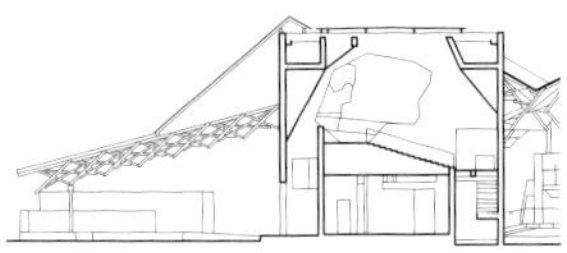

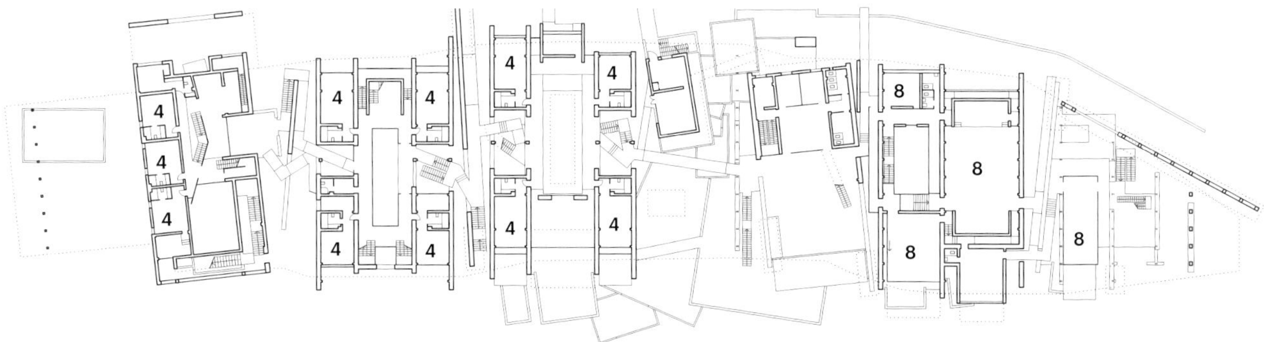

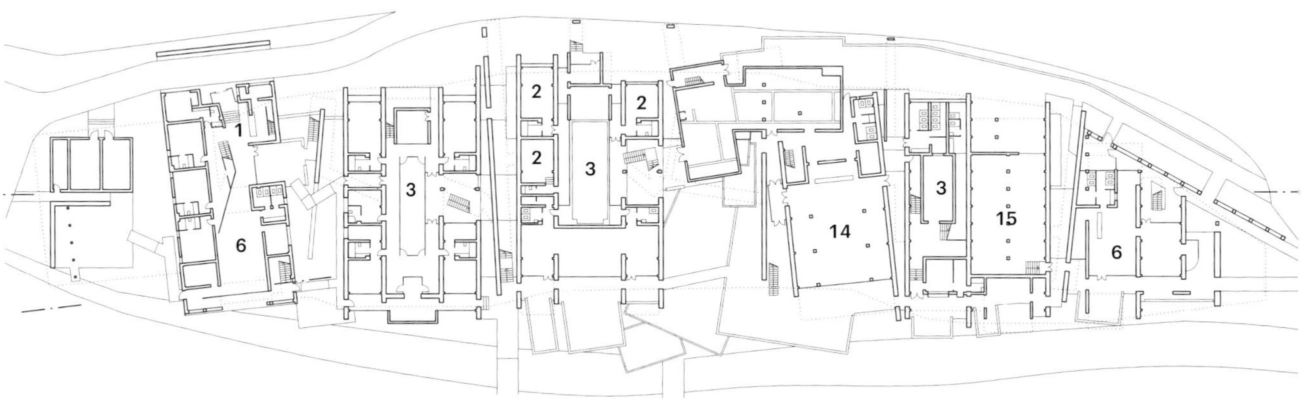

←BC AREA

Loft-Apartments mit Stil

Stylish Loft Flats

Charmante Loft-Apartments im Retrostil bietet das Yu Hotel in Shanghai. Nicht weit vom South Bund entfernt, befindet es sich ganz in der Nähe des berühmten Hotels The Waterhouse von Neri&Hu in einer Gegend, die immer mehr zum Szeneviertel avanciert. Entstanden ist das kleine Gästehaus durch den Umbau von zwei niedrigen, in Form und Material sehr unterschiedlichen Gebäuden an einem engen Hof, die zuvor schon teilweise als Hostel dienten und die nun eine moderne Fassade aus Metall und Glas zusammenbindet.
Die eigenwillig gestalteten und komplett durchgestylten Gästezimmer werden von warmen Brauntöne geprägt, die von dem dunklen Holz der Möblierung ebenso herrühren wie von einigen Zutaten aus Kupfer und Messing, beispielsweise den extravaganten Halterungen für Schminkspiegel und Leuchten. Nichts ist hier dem Zufall überlassen, jedes noch so kleine Accessoire ist von den Designern entworfen oder auswählt. Im Obergeschoss verleiht die sichtbare, industriell anmutende Dachkonstruktion aus Holz den Räumen eine besondere Note. Auch die Grundrisse sind alle individuell, zwei besonders großzügig angelegte Apartments verfügen über eine eigene Schlafgalerie. Mit seinem geschmackvoll inszenierten Loft-Charakter trifft das Yu Hotel exakt das Lebensgefühl einer neuen Mittelschicht in China.

The Yu Hotel in Shanghai offers charming, retro-style loft flats. Not far from the South Bund, it is also located close to the famous hotel The Waterhouse by Neri&Hu, in an area that is increasingly becoming a trendy neighbourhood. The small guesthouse was created by converting two low-rise buildings next to a narrow courtyard, which are very different in terms of their shape and material, and had previously already partly served as a hostel, and which are now tied together by modern facades of metal and glass.
The idiosyncratic and highly stylish guestrooms are characterised by warm shades of brown, deriving from both the dark wood of the furniture and some touches of copper and brass, such as the extravagant mounts for make-up mirrors and lamps. Nothing has been left to chance here, and every small accessory has been designed or selected by the designers. On the upper floor, the exposed, industrial-looking timber roof construction lends the spaces a special flavour. The floor plans, too, are all individual, while two spaciously arranged flats have their own sleeping gallery. With its tastefully orchestrated loft character, the Yu Hotel precisely meets the attitude to life of a new middle class in China.

Ort: Shanghai
Architekten: Shanghai Ben Zhe Architecture Design
Bauherr: Yu Hotel
Zimmer: 12

Location: Shanghai
Architects: Shanghai Ben Zhe Architecture Design
Client: Yu Hotel
Rooms: 12

Grundriss	Floor Plan
Maßstab 1:400	scale 1:400
1 Empfang/ Rezeption/Lobby	1 Front desk/ Reception/Lobby
2 Restaurant	2 Restaurant
3 Hof	3 Courtyard
4 Gästezimmer	4 Guestroom

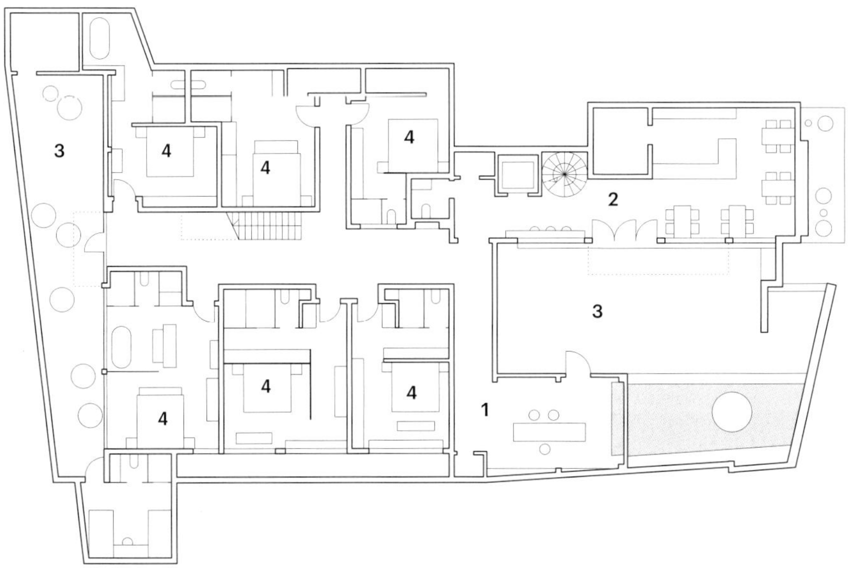

渝舍印象

Architekturjuwel in fantastischer Lage

Architectural Gem in a Fantastic Location

Vom Liegestuhl am Swimmingpool streift der Blick über den mäandernden Fluss und die pittoresken Karstberge im Abenddunst. Im Alila Yangshuo ist man mittendrin in einer der berühmtesten Landschaften Chinas, einem wahren Sehnsuchtsort. Doch nicht nur die einmalige Lage fasziniert, sondern auch die Architektur – der ausdrucksstarke und sensibel wiederhergerichtete Bestand einer ehemaligen Zuckermühle ebenso wie die edel gestalteten und gefühlvoll eingefügten Neubauten mit den Gästezimmern und Luxusapartments außenherum oder die sorgfältig angelegten Freiflächen dazwischen.
Die Hotelzimmer selbst sind sehr klar und zurückhaltend eingerichtet. Alle Aufmerksamkeit wird über großflächige Fenster auf die Umgebung gelenkt oder in die üppig begrünten Höfe der Suiten mit ihrem verschwenderischen Platzangebot. Wenige, gezielt ausgewählte Accessoires stellen immer wieder Bezüge zum Ort und seiner Vergangenheit her. Sinnlicher und mehr als Erlebnis inszeniert zeigen sich die halböffentlichen Räume in den äußerlich unveränderten Altbauten. Das beginnt mit der Rezeption und Lobby im ehemaligen Kraftwerk, wo eine knallrote, in den Boden eingelassene runde Sitzgruppe alle Blicke auf sich zieht, geht weiter über den Pressraum, der jetzt eine moderne Bar und mehr als hundert Rumsorten beherbergt bis hin zum Sugarhouse Restaurant im früheren Raffineriegebäude. Raue Oberflächen aus strukturiertem Beton und rostendem Stahl unterstreichen hier den industriellen Charme und lassen Alt und Neu zu einer harmonischen Einheit verschmelzen.

From a beach chair at the swimming pool, the view passes over the meandering river and the picturesque karst mountains in the evening mist. The Alila Yangshuo is right in the middle of one of the most famous landscapes in China a true place of yearning. However, not only the unique location is fascinating, the architecture is too – the expressive and sensitively renovated building stock, comprising a former sugar mill, just as the exquisitely designed and delicately incorporated new buildings with the guestrooms and luxury flat on the outside, or the carefully arranged open areas in between.
The hotel rooms themselves have been furnished in a very clear and reserved manner. The large windows draw all attention to the surroundings or to the lavishly greened courtyards of the suites with their extravagant space. A small number of specifically selected accessories repeatedly establishes relationships with the place and its history. The semi-public spaces in the externally unchanged old buildings appear more sensual, having been choreographed more to create an experience. Beginning with the reception and the lobby in the former power plant, where a bright red, round seating area embedded in the floor attracts all attention, this is carried on in the pressing room, which now houses a modern bar and more than a hundred types of wine, and continues in the Sugarhouse Restaurant in the former refinery building. Here, rough surfaces of structured concrete and rusting steel highlight the industrial charm, allowing the old and the new to merge in harmonious unity.

Ort: Yangshuo/Guangxi
Architekten: Gong Dong/Vector Architects
Innenarchitekten: Bin Ju/Horizontal Space Design
Bauherr: Landmark Tourism Investment Company
Zimmer: 177

Location: Yangshuo/Guangxi
Architects: Gong Dong/Vector Architects
Interior architects: Bin Ju/Horizontal Space Design
Client: Landmark Tourism Investment Company
Rooms: 177

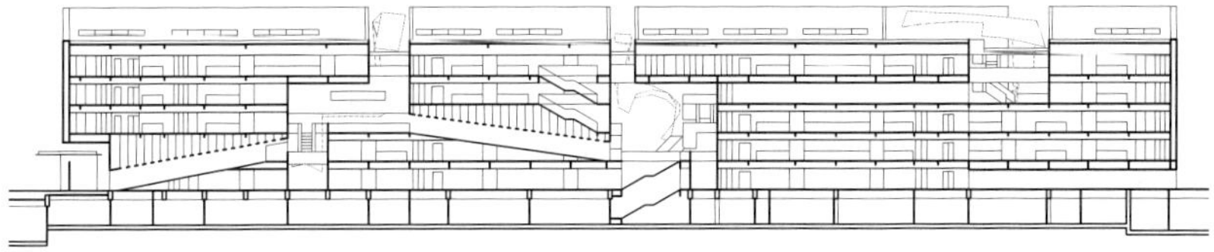

Schnitt/Grundriss
Maßstab 1:1250
1 Rezeption/Lobby
2 Restaurant
4 Gästezimmer
5 Suite
9 Bibliothek
10 Spa
11 Swimmingpool
16 Pool Villa

Section/Floor Plan
scale 1:1,250
1 Reception/Lobby
2 Restaurant
4 Guestroom
5 Suite
9 Library
10 Wellness
11 Swimming pool
16 Pool Villa

Architektur für das besondere Erlebnis: Im Gespräch mit Vector Architects

Architecture for a Special Experience: In Conversation with Vector Architects

Frank Kaltenbach:
Sie sind einer der wichtigsten Vertreter der jungen Generation chinesischer Architekten, die zwar im Ausland studiert und gearbeitet hat, nun aber mit dem eigenen Büro von China aus international auf sich aufmerksam macht. Neben dem Alila Yangshuo Hotel wurden die Bibliothek am Meer oder das Captain's House weltweit publiziert. All diese Bauten liegen an landschaftlich reizvollen Orten. Woran liegt das?

Gong Dong:
Von der Bibliothek sind nur Fotos bekannt, auf denen das Gebäude komplett frei am Strand steht. In dieser Isolation wirkt sie sehr ästhetisch, aber auch etwas skurril. Tatsächlich wollte der Investor mit dem Bau als Stadtteilbibliothek seine neue große Wohnsiedlung aufwerten, um sein Image zu verbessern. Diese Siedlung ist inzwischen fertig gebaut, Sie würden den Ort nicht wiedererkennen: Die Ferienhäuser rücken dicht an die Bibliothek heran.

Das Captain's House ist im Rahmen einer Fernsehserie entstanden. Die Aufgabe lautete für bekannte Architekten, die Wohnungen ausgewählter Familien attraktiver zu gestalten. In meinem Fall fand ich es sinnvoll, das alte Haus des wichtigsten Fischers im Dorf aufzustocken. Mit dem Tonnendach aus Sichtbeton erweckt es nun den Eindruck eines kompletten Neubaus. Die Sendung wurde in ganz China ausgestrahlt und hat viel zu meiner Popularität beigetragen. Ganz sicher spielt dabei auch die spektakuläre Lage auf der Halbinsel im Meer eine Rolle.

FK Bevorzugen Sie solche kleine Aufgaben vor Landmark Buildings in den Metropolen?

GD Natürlich würden wir auch gern in den großen Städten bauen. Aber gerade für die junge Architektengeneration ist es sehr schwierig, dort Aufträge zu bekommen, meistens sind es ganz kleine Projekte. Wer als unabhängiger Architekt in China bauen möchte, muss immer mit einem

Sanierung und Aufstockung Captain's House auf einer Halbinsel bei Fuzhou.

Renovation of and addition of floors in Captain's House on a peninsula near Fuzhou.

Frank Kaltenbach:
You are one of the most prominent figures of a young generation of Chinese architects who have studied and worked abroad but are now attracting international attention with their own studios in China. The Alila Yangshuo Hotel, the Seashore Library and the Captain's House have been written about all over the world. Each of these buildings is in a picturesque setting. Why is that?

Dong Gong:
The Library is usually depicted in a way that makes it look like the building was placed on the seashore all by itself. This supposed isolation gives it a highly aesthetic but also slightly whimsical appearance. The fact is, the investor wanted to build a neighbourhood library to make his large, new housing development more attractive and to enhance its image. The development is now complete, and you wouldn't recognise the place: the holiday homes are really close to the Library.
The Captain's House was created as part of a TV series. The task was for well-known architects to give the flats of selected families a makeover. In my case, I found it useful to build an additional storey onto the old house of the village's leading fisherman, and so the project turned into a real building. The programme aired all over China and contributed much to my popularity. The building's spectacular situation on a peninsula in the sea surely had a part in that.

FK Do you prefer such small tasks to landmark buildings in the metropolises?

GD Of course we would also like to build in the big cities. But especially for the younger generation of architects it is very difficult to get commissions there, we are usually offered only very small projects. Anyone who wants to build as an independent architect in China must always work with a state-owned design institute, whether he comes from abroad or has his studio in China. Hence we rely on private clients and only stand a chance where the state considers a project to be of little significance: in the countryside or in the suburbs. When you have made a name for yourself, you will get opportunities in the cities – we are now working on our first projects for a university campus.

FK You have been building hotels in China for about 15 years. How has this building task changed in the meantime?

GD At that time, there was mainly demand for five-star business hotels. Then, ten years ago, a boom in holiday hotels set in all over China, which remains unbroken until today.

FK What is the reason for that?

GD Many people now have more money to spend. At the same time, they work much more and wish to recover from their stressful lives in the big cities at least for a weekend.

FK Does that also explain the boom of rural hotels and the revival of traditional craftsmanship?

GD For a long time, all capital went to the big cities and, consequently, a large part of the rural population also migrated there. Rural areas dropped behind as a result. Five years ago, people then started to become more interested in remote rural areas and their cultural heritage. The villages there are increasingly being renovated, providing beautiful images in picturesque landscapes. But we have to be careful that the new buildings or refurbishments are not only used for the urban population's consumerist purposes. Many of these places will die away if nobody invests in the right uses.

FK Isn't there a trend towards local construction materials and local agricultural products, as in rural areas in Europe?

GD The more hotels are built, the more they must develop their own distinctive profile. Specialisation in regional cuisine is an essential factor, particularly when it comes to addressing guests from abroad. And that will also benefit the rural population.

FK As with your organic farm near Kunshan?

GD The organic farm was in fact a project in which we could not yet contribute to the improvement of village structures. That was eight years ago, rural areas had not yet become the focus of interest they are today. We were able to build a small

staatlichen Designinstitut zusammenarbeiten, ganz gleich, ob er aus dem Ausland kommt oder in China sein Büro hat. Wir sind also auf private Auftraggeber angewiesen und kommen nur dort zum Zug, wo das Projekt nach Einschätzung des Staats keine große Bedeutung hat: auf dem Land oder in den Suburbs. Erst wenn man sich einen Namen gemacht hat, erhält man auch in den Städten Aufträge, wir haben dort die ersten Projekte auf einem Hochschulcampus.

FK Sie bauen seit etwa 15 Jahren Hotels in China. Was hat sich seither bei dieser Bauaufgabe verändert?

GD Damals waren vor allem Fünf-Sterne-Businesshotels gefragt. Vor zehn Jahren setzte dann in ganz China dieser Boom an Ferienhotels ein, der bis heute ungebrochen ist.

FK Wie erklären Sie sich das?

GD Viele Leute haben inzwischen mehr Geld zum Ausgeben zur Verfügung. Gleichzeitig arbeiten sie viel mehr und wollen sich vom Stress in den großen Städten zumindest für ein Wochenende erholen.

FK Kommen daher auch der Boom der vielen Hotels auf dem Land und das Revival handwerklicher Tradition?

GD Lange Zeit ging das gesamte Kapital in die großen Städte und auch ein Großteil der Landbevölkerung ist dorthin abgewandert. Der ländliche Raum ist dadurch stark zurückgefallen. Seit den letzten fünf Jahren interessieren sich die Leute auch für abgelegenere Gegenden auf dem Land und deren kulturelles Erbe. Wir müssen aber aufpassen, dass die Neubauten oder Sanierungen dort nicht nur für den Konsum der Stadtbevölkerung genutzt werden. Zwar werden zunehmend die Dörfer dort hübsch renoviert und liefern schöne Bilder in einer malerischen Landschaft. Das sollte aber nicht darüber hinwegtäuschen, dass viele Orte aussterben, wenn niemand in die richtigen Nutzungen investiert.

FK Gibt es nicht wie in den ländlichen Gegenden in Europa auch einen Trend hin zu lokalen Baumaterialien und lokalen landwirtschaftlichen Produkten?

GD Je mehr Hotels dieser Art entstehen, desto mehr müssen sie ihr eigenes, unverwechselbares Profil entwickeln. Eine Spezialisierung auf regionale Küche ist dabei ein wesentlicher Faktor, vor allem auch wenn es darum geht, Gäste aus dem Ausland anzusprechen. Und davon wird dann auch die Landbevölkerung profitieren.

FK Wie bei Ihrer Ökofarm in Kunshan?

GD Die Ökofarm ist eben genau so ein Projekt, bei dem wir noch nicht zur Verbesserung dörflicher Strukturen beitragen konnten. Das war vor acht Jahren, damals stand der ländliche Raum noch nicht so im Fokus des Interesses wie heute. Immerhin konnten wir in dem landwirtschaftlich genutzten Garten eines Ausflugshotels, das im Einzugsgebiet von Shanghai liegt, ein kleines Gebäude errichten, der Begriff Ökofarm ist allerdings etwas übertrieben. Noch länger liegt unser Hotelentwurf für das Projekt Ordos 100 zurück, das von Herzog & de Meuron und Ai Wei Wei kuratiert wurde: eine kleine Siedlung aus hundert Häusern am Rand der Hauptstadt der Inneren Mongolei. Jedes dieser Gebäude sollte von einem anderen internationalen jungen Architekturbüro gebaut werden. Wir planten ein Hotel als Hochhaus. Das Gesamtprojekt wurde jedoch eingestellt.

FK Worin besteht für Sie der Reiz, ein Hotel zu planen, im Vergleich zu anderen Bauaufgaben?

GD Ich glaube, man muss sich als Architekt eher die Frage stellen, worin der Unterschied zwischen einem Businesshotel liegt und einem Resort. Ein Businesshotel wird meist wegen seiner günstigen Lage oder des günstigen Preises in der gewünschten Kategorie gebucht, nicht wegen seiner Architektur. An ein Hotel, in dem man mit seiner Familie oder Freunden privat ein Wochenende oder seine Ferien verbringt, stellen die Gäste ganz andere Erwartungen: Sie suchen eine Architektur, die ihnen etwas Besonderes bietet, was sie nicht im Alltag erleben können. Sie suchen eine ansprechende Umgebung, um abschalten zu können.

Bibliothek zwischen Wellen und Sand: Die Seashore Library in Beidaihe bietet faszinierende Ausblicke auf das Meer.

A library with a backdrop of waves and sand: the Seashore Library in Beidaihe offers fascinating views of the sea.

FK Gibt es da einen Unterschied zwischen China und anderen Ländern?

GD In China sind solche Ferienhotels eine Entwicklung der letzten Jahre. Oft bleiben die Gäste nur wenige Tage, aber der Aufenthalt in einem Hotel ist zum festen Bestandteil im Lifestyle des neuen Mittelstands geworden.

FK Wie sieht dieser Lifestyle im Alila Yangshuo Hotel konkret aus?

GD Der Name Alila bedeutet übersetzt »Überraschung«. Man möchte also keinen Mainstream bieten, sondern eine Entschleunigung auf ganz besondere Art. Das betrifft Aktivitäten, das Essen, vor allem aber die Architektur.

FK Wie haben Sie diese Zielvorgabe bei Ihrem Entwurf umgesetzt?

GD So viel mussten wir gar nicht erfinden, denn die Ausgangssituation war denkbar günstig – eine wundervolle Natur mit viel Wasser und die beeindruckenden Ziegelbauten der stillgelegten Zuckermühle. Diese Gestaltungselemente reichen allein schon aus, um sich von üblichen Hotelneubauten abzusetzen. Für mich war es einfacher, diese Energie des Orts in meinen Ergänzungen aufzunehmen, als von ganz vorne neu zu entwerfen.

FK Worin sehen Sie die besonderen Qualitäten?

GD Ich denke, es ist uns gelungen, eine harmonische Atmosphäre zwischen Alt und Neu herzustellen. Das Überraschungsmoment lässt sich auf vielen unterschiedlichen Ebenen erleben. Zum Beispiel ermöglichen die außen liegenden Treppen einen direkten Blick auf die nahen Felsen, während vom Swimmingpool der Blick weit über den Fluss schweifen kann. Früher sind hier die Boote mit dem Zuckerrohr der umliegenden Felder angelandet, vielleicht spürt man das noch heute.

FK Konnten Sie alle Ihre Vorstellungen beim Bauherrn durchzusetzen?

GD Obwohl die Investoren reine Finanzspezialisten sind, bewiesen sie einen sehr guten architektonischen Geschmack und ließen sich von meinen Vorschlägen zu Raumqualitäten, Material oder Detailausbildungen überzeugen. Vor allem hatten aber alle beteiligten Vertreter der unterschiedlichen Partner ein klar formuliertes Ziel. Das machte Entscheidungen im Vergleich zu Budgetverhandlungen mit anderen Bauherren ungewöhnlich einfach.

FK Können Sie ein Beispiel nennen?

GD Es ist nicht selbstverständlich, dass der Betreiber eines Ferienhotels den Zimmertrakt direkt an eine vielbefahrene Straße setzt. Der Bauherr hat aber verstanden, dass wir nur dadurch einen wunderbaren lärmgeschützten Garten zwischen dem Neubau und einer wild bewachsenen Felswand gewinnen, der dem schmalen Grundstück eine hohe Aufenthaltsqualität verleiht. Zur Straße hin haben wir dann einen Laubengang gelegt und mit einem perforierten Mauerwerk einen Filter vorgehängt.

FK Auch die Verwendung von Sichtbeton ist in chinesischen High-End-Hotels eher unüblich.

GD Der Bauherr hat verstanden, dass Beton den industriellen Charakter des Bestands unterstreicht. Es ist ja auch ein ganz besonderer Beton – zumindest was die Hohlsteine vor den Laubengängen und Loggien betrifft.

FK Wie konnten Sie diese hohe Präzision mit nur 25 Millimeter dünnen Wandstärke erreichen?

GD Wir haben viele Musterwände mit unterschiedlichsten Steinformaten ausprobiert. Als wir schließlich das optimale Verhältnis zwischen Sichtschutz, Ausblick und Tragverhalten ermittelt hatten, fanden wir keine Firma, die so eine Präzision in faserbewehrtem Beton umsetzen kann. Der Bauherr hat schließlich selbst auf der Baustelle eine kleine Feldfabrik eingerichtet und neun bis zehn Arbeiter angestellt, die über die gesamte Bauzeit hinweg die Steine von Hand mit einer selbst entwickelten Maschine gepresst haben.

building in the agriculturally used garden of a hotel for day-trippers, located in the catchment area of Shanghai – but it would be exaggerating to call it an organic farm. Our hotel design for the Ordos 100 project curated by Herzog & de Meuron and Ai Wei Wei dates back even further: a small development of a hundred buildings on the edge of the capital of Inner Mongolia. Each of these buildings was to be designed by a different young, international architectural practice. We came up with plans for a high-rise hotel. The whole project was however discontinued.

FK What is the appeal of designing a hotel compared to other building tasks?

GD I believe that, for an architect, the more interesting question is in the difference between a business hotel and a resort. People will book a room at a business hotel thanks to its convenient location or low price in the desired category, not because of its design. When it comes to a hotel where you spend your weekend or holiday with family or friends, guests have entirely different expectations: they are looking for architecture offering something special that they cannot experience in everyday life. They are looking for an appealing environment to help them unwind.

FK Is China different from other countries in that respect?

GD In China, these holiday hotels are a development of recent years. Guests will often stay for only a few days, but hotels have become an integral part of the new middle class's lifestyle.

FK How is this lifestyle expressed at the Alila Yangshuo Hotel?

GD The name Alila translates as 'surprise'. The hotel's aim is not to offer mainstream amenities but a very special form of deceleration. This concerns activities, the food and, above all, the architecture.

FK How did you implement this objective in your design?

GD We actually didn't have to come up with too many ideas, since the initial situation was extremely favourable – surrounded by wonderful nature with lots of water and the decommissioned sugar mill's impressive brick buildings. These design elements already contain more than enough to set you apart from the usual new hotel buildings. It was easier for me to incorporate the place's spirit into my additions than to design something new from scratch.

FK Where do you see its special qualities?

GD I think we have succeeded in creating a harmonious coexistence of old and new. The element of surprise can be experienced on many different levels. For example, the outside staircases provide a direct view of the nearby rocks, while the swimming pool offers views of the river and beyond. In the past, boats with sugar cane from the surrounding fields landed here – maybe you can still feel it today.

FK Did the clients support all your ideas?

GD The investors are financial specialists, but they showed very good architectural taste and I was able to convince them of my suggestions for spatial qualities, material and detailed solutions. Above all, however, all the representatives of the different partners involved had a clearly formulated goal. This made decisions as compared to budget negotiations with other clients unusually easy.

FK Can you give an example?

GD It is not self-evident that a holiday hotel operator will put the room wing directly on a busy street. However, the client understood that we would gain a wonderful, noise-protected garden between the new building and a wildly overgrown rock face, which gives the narrow property a high quality of stay. We put an arcade on the street face, with perforated masonry acting as a screen.

FK Exposed concrete is also rather uncommon in Chinese high-end hotels.

GD The client understood that concrete would underline the existing buildings' industrial character. It is also a very special concrete – at least as far as

FK Jede zweite Steinreihe besteht aus massiven Natursteinen, weshalb?

GD Diese weißen Bashi-Steine kommen aus der Region, werden dort häufig verbaut und sind sehr kostengünstig. Wir haben sie ganz scharf zugeschnitten, sodass ihre grüne Maserung zum Vorschein kommt. Mit der Zeit werden sie unter der Bewitterung aber den grauen Farbton des Betons annehmen. Dann muss man schon sehr nahe an die Mauern treten, um den Unterschied zwischen künstlichem Stein und Naturstein zu sehen. So subtile Unterschiede mag ich sehr.

FK Was am Alila Hotel Yangshuo würden Sie als typisch chinesisch bezeichnen?

GD Mit dem Begriff »typisch chinesisch« sollte man sehr vorsichtig umgehen. China ist ein großes Land mit mehr als 50 verschiedenen Völkern und unterschiedlichen Kulturen.

FK Was ist also typisch für den ganz speziellen Kontext in Yangshuo?

GD In gewisser Weise die Gartengestaltung, die linearen, versetzt angeordneten Steinplatten oder die Beziehung zwischen künstlichen Räumen und der Natur. Um den Bezug zur Natur zu intensivieren, haben wir zwei getrennte Erschließungssysteme: Der Laubengang, der die Zimmer mit den Aufzügen verbindet, verläuft schnurgerade, während ein zweiter Erschließungsweg vielfältige räumliche Erlebnisse und Ausblicke bietet – mit überdachten außen liegenden Treppen unter gefalteten Bambusschirmen. Beide Erschließungen sind in gewisser Weise durch die alten Wege in den steilen Kalkfelsen inspiriert. Sie wirken auch im Alila Yangshuo wie aus dem Fels gemeißelt. Solche Referenzen ergeben sich aber eher unbewusst beim Entwerfen aus dem konkreten Kontext, nicht weil ich a priori eine chinesische Architektur machen möchte. Mir war wichtig, die Horizontalität des Gartens und die spiegelnde Wasserfläche mit einem vertikalen Weg durch das Gebäude zu verbinden. Dennoch sollte sich der Neubau dem Bestand unterordnen und nicht mit zu vielen gestalterischen Themen spielen.

FK Sie haben sich ganz auf die Architektur konzentriert, während den gesamten Innenausbau Bin Ju von Horizontal Space Design entworfen hat. Wie war Ihre Zusammenarbeit?

GD Bin Ju ist ein guter Freund von mir. Beim Alila Yangshuo ist er der Interior Designer, aber auch einer der sieben Investoren. Das bedeutet, er ist auch mein Bauherr. Bevor ich in das Projekt involviert war, hatten bereits zwei andere Architekturbüros zwei Jahre lang entworfen, ihre Vorschläge waren aber immer wieder von den Partnern abgelehnt worden. Deshalb fragte mich Bin Ju, ob ich nicht als Architekt einsteigen wolle. Als ich zum ersten Mal auf dem Grundstück stand, hatte ich mich sofort in die alte Fabrik verliebt und sagte zu. In der Planungsphase hatten wir dann das übliche Verhältnis zwischen Architekt und Innenarchitekt. Dieser Prozess ist sehr einvernehmlich verlaufen. Wir haben uns natürlich öfter ausgetauscht, aber jeder hat seinen Teil für sich bearbeitet. Ich finde seinen Innenausbau sehr zurückhaltend und gut auf meine Architektur abgestimmt. Innenarchitekten lassen sich vielleicht eher von Trends und Moden leiten als Architekten. Für ein Hotel ist das passend und in diesem speziellen Fall sehr gut gelungen.

FK Worin hat sich Ihre Arbeit am Alila Yangshuo von Ihren anderen Bauprojekten in China unterschieden?

GD Von dem Zeitpunkt, an dem ich in das Projekt involviert war, bis zur Eröffnung vergingen beinahe fünf Jahre. Für China ist das eine lange Zeit, normalerweise möchten Investoren ihr Geld schneller zurück und genehmigen keine aufwendigen Studien für Konstruktionsdetails oder Materialforschungen. Auch der Bauherrenvertreter der Alila-Gruppe war äußerst anspruchsvoll, was die Qualität des Entwurfs und der Ausführung betrifft. Obwohl wir wirklich mit vielen konstruktiven Lösungen gekämpft haben, hat der Auftraggeber nie von uns verlangt, unsere Idee zu ändern oder auf eine einfachere Lösung auszuweichen. Bei vielen meiner anderen Projekte würde ich mir das auch wünschen.

the hollow bricks in front of the arcades and loggias are concerned.

FK How did you achieve such high precision at just 25 mm wall thickness?

GD We tried many prototype walls with all sorts of different brick formats. When we had finally determined the best balance between privacy, views and structural behaviour, we could not find a company capable of translating such precision into fibre-reinforced concrete. The client himself finally set up a small field factory on the construction site and hired 9 to 10 workers who pressed the bricks by hand over the entire construction period, using a specially developed machine.

FK Every second row consists of solid natural stones. Why?

GD These white Bashi stones come from the region of the construction site, are often used there and inexpensive. We cut them very sharply, to reveal their green grain. Over time and with weathering they will however take on the concrete's grey shade. Then you will have to step very closely to the walls to see the difference between artificial stone and natural stone. I like subtle differences like this a lot.

FK What about the Alila Hotel Yangshuo is typically Chinese?

GD One should be very careful about describing something as typically Chinese. China is a large country with more than fifty different peoples and different cultures.

FK What is typical for the special context of Yangshuo then?

GD In a sense, the garden design or the linear staggered stone slabs or the relationship between artificial spaces and nature. We have two separate access ways in order to intensify the relationship with nature: the arcade that connects the rooms with the lift is dead straight, while a second access way offers a variety of different spatial experiences and views – with covered outside stairs under folded bamboo umbrellas. Both access ways are in a sense inspired by the old paths in the steep limestone cliffs. At the Alila Yangshuo, they also look like they were carved out of the rock . However, such references come about more accidentally when designing from the concrete context, not because I set out to create Chinese architecture. It was important to me to connect the horizontality of the garden and the water's reflecting surface with a vertical path through the building. But the new building was also meant to complement the existing structures and not to be too playfully creative.

FK You focussed completely on the architecture, while the entire interior was designed by Bin Ju from Horizontal Space Design. How did you work together?

GD Bin Ju is a good friend of mine. At the Alila Yangshuo, he is the interior designer but also one of the seven investors. That means he is also my client. Before I got involved in the project, two other architectural firms had already worked on designs for two years, but their proposals were repeatedly rejected by the partners. That's why Bin Ju asked me if I wanted to take on the role of the architect. When I first stood on the property, I fell in love with the old factory at once and said yes. In the planning stage, we then had the usual relationship between architect and interior designer. This process was very amicable. Of course, we talked frequently, but we each focussed on our own part. I find his interior design very restrained and well adapted to my architecture. Interior designers may be more likely to follow trends and fashions than architects. For a hotel, that is suitable and very well done in this particular case.

FK How was your work on the Alila Yangshuo different from other building projects in China?

GD From the time I got involved in the project until the opening, almost five years passed. For China, this is a long time, usually investors want to get their money back faster and do not allow elaborate studies for design details or materials research. And the client representative of the Alila Group was also extremely demanding in terms of quality of design and execution. Although we really struggled over many constructive solutions, the client never asked us to change our idea or switch to a simpler solution. I would like that approach for many of my other projects, too.

CHRISTIAN SCHITTICH
studierte Architektur an der Technischen Universität München. Nach einigen Jahren Büropraxis und publizistischer Tätigkeit wechselte er 1991 in die Redaktion Detail, die er 25 Jahre lang leitete – zunächst als verantwortlicher Redakteur und ab 1998 als Chefredakteur. In dieser Zeit entwickelte sich Detail zu einer der international führenden Fachzeitschriften für Architekten und Bauingenieure.
Christian Schittich ist Autor und Herausgeber zahlreicher Fachartikel und Bücher. Seit August 2016 arbeitet er als freier Publizist und Fachautor.

FRANK KALTENBACH
schloss sein Architekturstudium an der Universität Stuttgart und der Arizona State University in Phönix, USA mit Diplom ab und arbeitete in namhaften Architekturbüros in Stuttgart, Tokio, Wien und München.
Seit 1998 ist er Redakteur der internationalen Architekturzeitschrift Detail und war unter anderem an deren Weiterentwicklung mit den Ausgaben von Detail Konzept und Detail Green sowie der italienischen Sprachausgabe beteiligt. Er ist Herausgeber des Bandes Transluzente Materialien aus der Reihe Detail Praxis.
Frank Kaltenbach lehrt seit 2007 an der Akademie der Bildenden Künste München das Fach Architektur- und Designgeschichte. Zu den Themen Architektur, Städtebau und Design publiziert er als Gastautor, hält Vorträge und moderiert Fachveranstaltungen.

CHRISTIAN SCHITTICH
studied architecture at the Technical University of Munich. After several years of office experience and journalistic work he joined the Detail editing team in 1991, which he headed for 25 years – initially as senior editor and from 1998 editor-in-chief. During this time, Detail became one of the leading international specialist journals for architects and civil engineers.
Christian Schittich is the author and editor of numerous specialist articles and books. Since August 2016, he has been working as freelance publicist and specialist author.

FRANK KALTENBACH
completed his studies of architecture at the University of Stuttgart and the Arizona State University in Phoenix, USA, graduating with a Diplom degree, and has worked in acclaimed architecture firms in Stuttgart, Tokyo, Vienna, and Munich.
Since 1998, he has been editor of the international professional journal DETAIL, and has contributed, amongst other things, to its further development with the Detail Konzept and Detail Green issues as well as the Italian-language issue. He is editor of the volume Transluzente Materialien [Translucent materials] in the DETAIL Praxis series.
Frank Kaltenbach has been teaching architectural and design history at the Academy of Fine Arts in Munich since 2007. He publishes as guest author, holds lectures, and moderates specialist events on the topics of architecture, urban development, and design.

Wuyuan Skywells Hotel
Yan village, Wuyuan, Jiangxi Province

Pingtian Cloud Village Hotel
Pingtian Village, Songyang County,
Zhejiang Province

Tsingpu Tulou Retreat
Taxia Village, Nanjing County,
Zhangzhou Town, Fujian

XY Yun House
Yangjia Village, Xingping Town,
Guangxi Province

Anadu Hotel
Moganshan, Huzhou, Zejiang

Luoqi Xitang Village B&B Hotel
Guojiagou, Tianjin Province

Daoming Bamboo Craft Village
Daoming County, Chongzhou City,
Sichuan Province

Sunyata Hotel
51, Yeyu South Road, 671000 Dali, Yunnan

Nashare Hotel
Huandao south road, Xiamen, Fujian Province

Hotel WIND
6#, Yunyue Mountian Villa, Huangcuo Road
Huandaogan Boulevard, Xiamen,
Fujian Province

sth.here
No. 14, Gongmenkou 2, Xicheng District, Beijing

Layering Courtyard Hutel
No. 159, Xi He Yan Street, Qianmen, Beijing

The Walled – Tsingpu Yangzhou Retreat
1 Baocheng Road, Hanjiang District, Yangzhou,
Jiangsu Province

The Waterhouse Boutique Hotel at South Bund
Maojiayuan Road 1–3, Huangpu District, Shanghai

Eight Tenths Garden
151 Yijia Road, Jiading District, Shanghai
Micro Hutong
53 Yang Mei Zhu Xiejie, Xicheng District, Beijing

Youth Hotel of iD Town
Fuzhong 3rd Rd., Shenzhen, Guangdong

Wa Shan – The Guesthouse on Xiangshan Campus
Xiangshan Campus, China Academy of Art,
Zhejiang, Hangzhou, Xihu, Zhuantang Straight St,
Hangzhou

Yu Hotel
439 East Fuxing Road, Shanghai

Alila Yangshuo Hotel
102 Dongling Road, Guilin, Guangxi Province

Allen, die durch Überlassung ihrer Bildvorlagen, durch Erteilung von Reproduktionserlaubnis und durch Auskünfte am Zustandekommen des Buches mitgeholfen haben, sagt der Verlag aufrichtigen Dank. Sämtliche Zeichnungen in diesem Werk sind eigens angefertigt oder stammen aus den Archiven der Architekten. Trotz intensiver Bemühungen konnten wir einige Urheber der Abbildungen nicht ermitteln, die Urheberrechte sind aber gewahrt. Wir bitten um dementsprechende Nachricht.

The publisher would like to express his sincere gratitude to all those who have assisted in the production of this book, be it through providing photos or artwork, or granting permission to reproduce their documents, or providing other information. All the drawings were specially produced for this publication or taken from the archives of the architects. Despite intensive endeavours, we were unable to establish copyright ownership in some cases; however, copyright is assured. Please notify us accordingly in such instances.

Fotografen/Photographers

Amateur Architecture Studio S. 16, 114, 117, 118
Bian Lin S. 58, 60–61, 62, 6
Chaos.Z S. 110, 112, 113
Chen Hao S. 124, 126, 129, Vorsatz/endpaper front
Christian Schittich S. 9 u., 12, 24 o., 26/27, 33, 41, 44 o.r., 47 o., 81, 108 o., 119
CreatAR Images (Luo Juncai)/Jin Weiqi S. 7, 82, 84, 85, 86/87, 100, 102, 104/105
Derryck Menere S. 94, 96, 98
He Bin S. 137 o.
Horizontal Design: Xufeng Jing S. 12, 127, 128
Huapeng Chu S. 63
Howard Chan S. 134
Jonathan Leijonhufvud/Zhaoyang Architects S. 64, 66, 67
Lei Mao S. 52, 54/55, 57
Marc Goodwin S. 20, 22, 23
Nacasa & Partners S. 72, 74, 75
Pedro Pegenaute S. 88, 90, 91, 92, 97, 99
SCHRAN Architectural Photography, Jin Xuanmin S. 120, 123
SU Shengliang S. 42, 44, 46, 47 u., 128 , 129, 130/131, 137 u.
Sven Zhang S. 48, 51
Tsingpu Tulou Retreat S. 34, 37, 38, 39, 40
Wang Haoran S. 28, 31, 32, 33
Wu Qingshan S. 106, 108 u., 109
Xia Zhi S. 24 u., 76, 78, 79, 80, 134, Nachsatz/endpaper back
Xu Xiaodong S. 68, 70, 71

Herausgeber/Editor
Christian Schittich

Autoren/Authors
Christian Schittich
Frank Kaltenbach (Interview)

Projektleitung/Project management
Eva Herrmann

Lektorat (Deutsch)/Copy editing (German)
Sandra Leitte

Übersetzung/Translation into English
Julian Jain

Lektorat (Englisch)/Copy editing (English)
Stefan Widdess

Gestaltung/Design
strobo B M

Illustration Cover/Cover illustration
Kai Meyer

Zeichnungen/Drawings
Ralph Donhauser

Herstellung, DTP/Production, DTP
strobo B M

Reproduktion/Reproduction
Ludwig:media gmbh

Druck und Bindung/Printing and binding
druckpruskil.gmbh

Die für dieses Buch verwendeten FSC-zertifizierten Papiere werden aus Fasern hergestellt, die nachweislich aus umwelt- und sozialverträglicher Herkunft stammen.
The FSC-certified paper used for this book is manufactured from fibres originating from environmentally and socially compatible sources.

MIX
Papier aus verantwortungsvollen Quellen
FSC® C014340
www.fsc.org

DETAIL – Detail Business Information GmbH, München/Munich
detail.de

ISBN 978-3-95553-458-5 (Print)
ISBN 978-3-95553-459-2 (E-Book)

Bibliografische Information der Deutschen Nationalbibliothek: Die Deutsche Nationalbibliothek verzeichnet diese Publikation in der Deutschen Nationalbibliografie; detaillierte bibliografische Daten sind im Internet über http://dnb.d-nb.de abrufbar.

Bibliographical information published by the German National Library. The German National Library lists this publication in the Deutsche Nationalbibliografie; detailed bibliographical data are available on the Internet at http://dnb.d-nb.de.